THE BIBLE FOR A *SHIFTING* SECULAR AGE

"In an age of constricting secularity, a gasp for spiritual well-being can be heard across the land. Should we be surprised? It is to this issue pastor and lecturer Domenic Ruso writes *The Bible for a Shifting Secular Age*, an important issue to which younger generations are giving serious attention. His outline and content carefully help us understand this issue in clear and relevant ways. I recommend this critical handbook to help us navigate our lives through the moonscape of our secular age."

—BRIAN STILLER, global ambassador, World Evangelical Alliance

"Domenic Ruso has written a deeply important book about the most significant book in history. The Bible contains a vast world that many are intimidated by or misunderstand completely. In a rapidly shifting culture, we need guides who can help us re-examine how the ancient story of Scripture can anchor our world—and our lives. Dom is the kind of guide we all need. He is a scholar who writes compellingly and with an urgency we all should carry. I believe every follower of Jesus would do well to read this book."

—RICH VILLODAS, author of *The Narrow Path*

"With wisdom and insight, Domenic Ruso meets us at the intersection of the Bible's timeless truth and the pressing realities of today's secular age. Here, he offers a compelling vision of Scripture that is both relevant and transformative in a post-Christian world."

—BRYCE ASHLIN-MAYO, President of Ambrose University and author of *Digital Mission: A Practical Guide for Ministry Online*

"*The Bible for a Shifting Secular Age* examines and grapples with a positive way to engage Christianity with current secular culture and society. The author introduces readers to a new view of the Bible in conjunction with current values of autonomy and self-understanding, the key values of what Charles Taylor has called our authentic age. The book uses existing high-quality field and scholarly research to help inform Bible reading and practice. This book is extremely helpful for Christians and (aspiring) church leaders who are seeking to find their place and understanding in a modern world."

—SARAH WILKINS-LAFLAMME, author of *Religion, Spirituality and Secularity among Millennials: The Generation Shaping American and Canadian Trends*

"In *The Bible for a Shifting Secular Age*, Domenic Ruso masterfully explores how the Scriptures address our deepest longings in an age of rapid cultural change. Combining theological depth with practical insight, Ruso unveils the Bible as more than an ancient text—but as a living source of hope, spiritual renewal, and relational healing in our fractured world. A timely, inspiring, and transformative read."

—Ken Shigematsu, author of *Survival Guide for the Soul*

"The Bible is back in vogue as a talking point in culture. However, there are new challenges and complexities to navigate. Domenic outlines a creative approach that can help us embrace the opportunities without dumbing down on truth. This book combines theological depth and practical tools as a vital guide for anyone who wants to see the Bible transforming lives today."

—Andrew Ollerton, author of *The Bible Course*

The Bible for a *Shifting* Secular Age

Hearing the Truth You Need
for the Life You Are Meant to Live

DOMENIC RUSO

Foreword by CAREY NIEUWHOF

CASCADE *Books* • Eugene, Oregon

THE BIBLE FOR A SHIFTING SECULAR AGE
Hearing the Truth You Need for the Life You Are Meant to Live

Copyright © 2025 Domenic Ruso. All rights reserved. Except for brief quotations in critical publications or reviews, no part of this book may be reproduced in any manner without prior written permission from the publisher. Write: Permissions, Wipf and Stock Publishers, 199 W. 8th Ave., Suite 3, Eugene, OR 97401.

Cascade Books
An Imprint of Wipf and Stock Publishers
199 W. 8th Ave., Suite 3
Eugene, OR 97401

www.wipfandstock.com

PAPERBACK ISBN: 978-1-6667-8490-9
HARDCOVER ISBN: 978-1-6667-8491-6
EBOOK ISBN: 978-1-6667-8492-3

Cataloguing-in-Publication data:

Names: Ruso, Domenic. | Foreword by Carey Nieuwhof.

Title: The Bible for a shifting secular age : hearing the truth you need for the life you are meant to live / Domenic Ruso; foreword by Carey Nieuwhof.

Description: Eugene, OR: Cascade Books, 2025 | Includes bibliographical references.

Identifiers: ISBN 978-1-6667-8490-9 (paperback) | ISBN 978-1-6667-8491-6 (hardcover) | ISBN 978-1-6667-8492-3 (ebook)

Subjects: LCSH: Bible—Criticism, interpretation, etc. | Christian life—Biblical teaching. | Secularism. | Religion and culture.

Classification: BS511.3 R87 2025 (print) | BS511.3 (ebook)

Contents

Foreword ix
Acknowledgments xi

Introduction: A Secular Surprise 1

PART 1: *Handles for Navigating the Shifts of a Secular Age*

Chapter 1–Less Religion, More Spirituality 17
Chapter 2–Less Power, More Participation 36
Chapter 3–Less Telling, More Teaching 54

PART 2: *The Bible Heard as Living Words*

Chapter 4–From the Bible as a Manual to the Bible as a Compass 79
Chapter 5–From the Bible as a Textbook to the Bible as Inexhaustible Treasure 97
Chapter 6–From the Bible as a Rule Book to the Bible as a Guide for Restored Relationships 118

Epilogue–Equipping People for the Future: The Church and Our Leadership Crisis 137

Bibliography 155

Foreword

THE SECULAR LANDSCAPE BEFORE us isn't what many Christians expected.

I tell my American church leader friends that as a Canadian, it's like I'm from the future. Canada became a secular nation as I was growing up, so the only kind of ministry I've done is in a post-Christian or, increasingly, pre-Christian culture. In many ways, that's been a preview of what's happening in the US right now.

In a similar vein, this book is from the future.

Dom Ruso (a fellow Canadian) has been cutting his pastoral teeth for a decade in secular, progressive Canada. To his full credit, he planted a church a decade ago in some of the hardest soil there is in North America—the very nonreligious province of Quebec.

These field notes and observations are like a pair of glasses you can put on to help you see what's happening in America. And honestly, it's more complex than you'd expect.

Instead of hitting a wall of atheism, you'll find surprising pockets of spiritual openness. Rather than facing flat-out rejection of faith, you'll run into people who are done with institutions but are still asking the big questions. Dom nails it when he observes that we're facing "less religion, more spirituality" today.

What I love about Dom's approach is that he doesn't just complain about these changes or wish for the good old days (which weren't always that good). Instead, he gives you practical handles for navigating this new reality—shifting from telling to teaching, from power to participation, and rethinking how we present the Bible itself.

His take on the Bible really clicked for me. For too long, we've pitched Scripture as either a rule book or an instruction manual, then scratched our heads when people don't engage with it. Dom frames the Bible as more of a compass that guides people and as a treasure to discover rather than just a textbook to memorize. It's a fresh approach that still takes the gift of the Bible and its accuracy seriously, while connecting with today's spiritually curious. He also points out that the gospel leads to restored relationships, something our culture desperately needs.

Look, if Dom is seeing spiritual curiosity in Montreal of all places, there's hope for wherever you are.

As church leaders, we're facing what Dom correctly calls a leadership crisis—a moment that demands both biblical depth and adaptive leadership. The frameworks he offers aren't just theory; they've been tested in one of North America's toughest spiritual environments.

This book will challenge you. It'll probably push against some comfortable assumptions. But that's exactly what the church needs right now.

The Bible remains "living and active" in every age. Dom's work helps us figure out how its timeless truth might connect in fresh ways with our rapidly changing world.

Carey Nieuwhof,
Author, Podcaster, and Speaker

Acknowledgments

THERE IS SOMETHING SPECIAL about the people who believe in you first. As I worked on this project many of those people who believed in me first flashed through my mind. At times I wondered if they lied to me to not hurt my feelings. However, slowly it became clear that they were not lying, but they could see a burden that I was carrying, yet would take years to fully materialize.

To the team at Cascade, especially Michael Thompson and my editor Rodney Clapp, thank you for your support and wisdom on this first book.

To my many mentors and teachers, thank you for not ignoring dumb questions. Dr. David Neelands, your insights about the church, history, and our rich theological legacy will always be with me. To the late Dr. Pamela Bright, you were right, "There is a prophetic angst that pierces through the noise when we keep one foot in the church and one in the academy."

To fellow colleagues who encouraged me early in the project: Thank you for not saying, "Do we really need another book on the Bible?" Dr. James Bekkers, what a gift to call you friend all these years. The laughs kept us leading in tough times. Rich Villodas, thanks for making time to listen to early ideas about this book. Your thoughts were so helpful. I also want to thank Carey Nieuwhof, who made time to read the book, share encouraging comments, and provide a foreword that captured many of the feelings I felt as I wrote it.

To my family: Mom and Dad, no words will capture how your sacrifices opened doors for me that you never had the chance to walk through. My wife, Beverly, you will never know what your "believing in me first" has meant. I will never forget the time you said: "Babe, one day your book will be on display at this conference." That kept me going when some chapters were not coming together. To my boys, you inspire me every day to be a

ACKNOWLEDGMENTS

better dad, husband, and leader, who can equip your generation so that you can lead in ways my generation never thought possible.

Lastly, to the 180 Church family, and other churches who gave me room to develop, my prayer is that this book would stretch and inspire you to remember those you love who are being shaped by an emerging "secular" world. Remember, no one is beyond the reach of the One who "is not far from any one of us."

As you read, may you be drawn to read the Bible more carefully and consistently. Only then will you hear the living truth of God's wisdom that goes beyond our present struggles. May you sense the Holy Spirit pointing you to Jesus, the Eternal Word of God, who is with us until the very end of any age.

Introduction

A Secular Surprise

"You are bringing some strange ideas to our ears,
and we would like to know what they mean."—Acts 17:20

A GROWING CRISIS WE CAN NOT IGNORE

IN 1807 A BIBLE, published for missionary use in the Caribbean, revealed some shocking features. While it was on exhibit at the Museum of the Bible, observers got a glimpse showing how key passages were omitted. What was more startling was what was omitted. Passages and key stories highlighting hope and freedom were removed. For instance, the exodus, a foundational story of a God who hears the cries of his people and responds to set them free, is left out. Consequently, the very trajectory of hope at the core of the Bible was lost.

Scholars estimate that only 50 percent of the New Testament and even less of the Old Testament had been included in this Bible. It is fair to say that this "Bible," if you can even call it that, remains a neutered version of the whole truth used to reinforce injustice and oppression. This Bible is now known as the Slave Bible.[1]

When I heard this story, I felt a deep sense of sadness that soon turned to anger. Maybe you sense that as well. Questions soon flooded my mind:

"How could Christians do this?"

"Why would those who wanted to share about Jesus use the Bible in this way?"

"How could this happen?"

"Why was this acceptable?"

1. Rae, "How Christian Slaveholders Used the Bible."

While we may never know the answers, it is stories like this that highlight the crisis we find ourselves in. It is a brewing crisis related to misuses of the Bible and the hurdles this creates for engaging with an emerging secular age. It might shock you, but I think this crisis may be one of the best times to reclaim the importance of the Bible, even as we continue to hear stories that devalue the sacred and special ways the Bible is meant to guide us. This crisis, and its impact on how we view the Bible, requires our attention as our present secular culture reveals some surprising shifts. They are shifts that include an openness to faith, concerns about injustice, curiosity about God, and many more. Hence, it has never been so important to get serious about a God-honoring view of the Bible while courageously heeding the shifts of our present secular age. In so doing, I believe this may be the best time to reclaim that the Bible has much to say about some of our deepest human longings.

For the past few years, I have had a front row seat to the way our secular culture is shifting. These changes, as I describe below, will require revisiting long-held assumptions about the Bible and people in a secular culture. In my role as a pastor, a dad, a church planter, and a practical theologian I have sensed the complexities that await us. I am also surprised by the unexpected interest people have in God, spirituality, cultural expressions of faith, and the Bible. Moreover, we are seeing a secular culture revealing a shocking spiritual resurgence. This, mingled with accelerated change, political disruptions, and relational fragmentation, will require the living words of truth found in the Bible to be heard properly and as trustworthy for the life we are meant to live.

Recent books like *The Surprising Rebirth of Belief in God* are shedding light on some of the same issues I have noticed. Podcasts and movies also seem to be pointing to an unexpected shift we did not anticipate. People are open, curious, struggling, and longing for a life that holds together—wonder and hope in the face of pain and sadness. I have wondered: "Where will people go when they start to doubt their doubts in God?" We might be living at a time when the modern Western view of a secular culture is being rewritten.[2] Unfortunately, many may miss these shifts because they are entrenched in old models. These mental models have a default outlook to interpret the challenges of our secular age through a lens of fear and despair, blinding us to opportunities.

---

2. Berger, "Secularism in Retreat."

Introduction

Years ago, while still in seminary, I sat in a debate that erupted into a tense discussion about the apologetics needed to deal with "secular" *atheism*. It was a shock and disappointment when, upon graduation, very few people cared to discuss or argue about such issues. While I was ready with my debates notes, many had moved away from a sheer atheistic outlook on life. Surprisingly, people were not comfortable with describing themselves as atheists. Instead, they were ready and open to believe in many forms of spirituality that promised connection with numerous gods. While many committed Christians were prepared to go to battle against one type of secular world, another post-religious outlook was taking shape. As I will describe later, this post-religious approach was less like atheism and more like a new type of gnosticism exposing our deep hunger for better answers that would help us make sense of life. Gnosticism is a term that draws on inner spirituality mingled with diverse ideas about salvation, suffering, and the deeper significance of life. More on this later.

This book is one I wish I had when I started seeing the shifts from the front lines. I have been blessed to serve in diverse leadership settings, however I suddenly sensed that the shifts of this secular age seemed different and more complex than I had imagined. This book is about providing new tools that point to the special way that the Bible must guide us again. Reading it, I hope you will grow in your confidence as you adjust your view of a secular context you might find yourself in. For those who do not see the shifts yet, a tidal wave is coming. Moreover, my goal is to minimize a common confrontational attitude toward the world as we sense an old paradigm fading. This is possible as we return to the Bible and see anew how God has equipped his people for these types of moments of significant change.

At the outset I want to make clear that this is not a book about how to defend the Bible *against* the changes of a bad world that doesn't like Christians. In fact, that Bible wisely warns: "Do not say, 'Why were the old days better than these?' For it is not wise to ask such questions."[3] Instead, I believe a deeper appreciation for the Bible reduces fear so that we may seek to interpret what is happening in our culture in a way that models our trust in God and his living Word found in the Bible. At a time when many in our secular age equate the Bible with religious debates or philosophical/theological problems, we must look for new ways to explore and explain how the Bible is so much more than that. We may be surprised to see those

3. Eccl 7:10.

in a secular age open to the way the Bible calls us to authentic living, honest doubting, and a life-giving sense of purpose that reminds us that we are loved even when we do not feel it.

GETTING HONEST ABOUT CHANGE

The biblical framework we must explore has to do with what the Bible is, and why it remains trustworthy. When we can hear the truth about our broken world and how a loving God is relentless in restoring what is his, we start to see that we have a part to play as well. The pace of change and the disorientation of this cultural moment has caught many of us by surprise. If you have read the Bible, you know that God often uses surprises to awaken his followers to new things he is doing. For example, no one expected the shocking revelation that *the Truth* was to be understood as a person, fully embodied in Jesus.[4] Similarly, I am convinced that the more we read the Bible, the better equipped we should be when new changes and shifts come our way. This means that those who have read the Bible with consistency should be the least flustered when handling surprising shifts.

One of the early biographers of Jesus' life and ministry captured a mind-blowing truth fully embodied in a person when he stated, "Jesus was the *Word*, with God, from the beginning."[5] All that is to say that all other words in the Bible are meant to help us return to a faithful and accurate understanding of Jesus, the eternal Word of God who is the only reason we even have a Bible.[6]

A few weeks ago, we had over forty people gather at church to work their way through a Bible study. As part of that learning time, we kept affirming that a simplistic commentary on the Bible will not be enough to help us deal with the changes infused by secular values. Devotional pep talks are not enough for the surprises coming our way. What we will need is a fresh engagement with the Bible, and a robust understanding of what the Bible actually is that helps us navigate the complexities of our time.

I believe that my context is a harbinger of what is to come for North America and other parts of the world. Also, as a church leader on the front lines, I am noticing how ill-equipped long-time Christians are in navigating the shifts they face. A common pushback I hear seeks a simplistic

---

4. John 14:6.
5. John 1:1.
6. With reference to the New Testament.

Introduction

commentary to go back to Bible. Often what people mean is that we need to return to a time when everyone just agreed to embrace the Bible as *the Word of God*. To be honest, I can think of all the meetings where I wished that too. But that is not going to happen and a romantic view of some good old days will only set us back further. The habits and values of a secular age are here to stay.

Faith Today, a magazine that addresses faith issues in Canada, revealed that most Christians have slowly abandoned reading their Bibles. In the province of Quebec, noted to be one of the most complex secular spaces in North America, it is even more alarming. Although 51 percent of Canadians who define themselves as evangelical read the Bible regularly, there is a drastic drop to only 4 percent recorded for those living in Quebec.[7] If we can discern anything it is that the more secular a context gets, the less the Bible is seen as essential for growth, maturity, and ongoing spiritual vitality. This comes at a time when a secular age is surprising us with new interest in spiritual conversations. Further, this comes at a time when those do read the Bible detach it from the larger story of redemption and hope.

SECULAR + DIGITAL NATIVES[8]

For years I have also spent some time teaching in academic settings. I bring this up so you will know that my desire is to see a needed connection between practical learning and sustained theological reflection. A secular age will expose shallow thinking. Moreover, the shifts of our secular contexts will capitalize on a sectarian view of the Christian faith that is common within churches. As one family member once remarked: "To the outside world, Christianity can seem like a pluralistic religion." Unfortunately, it is a sad but true commentary that this will only accelerate in a digital age bent on fueling sectarian outlooks. It will be paramount to reimagine new ties between the academy and the practical streams of learning, while returning to the centrality of the Bible.

At their fingertips, digital natives will find countless clips, speakers and silly memes that make up our digital revolution. Therefore, insights related to the Bible cannot ignore technology and how digital tools will influence and impact the emerging secular age. Conversely, there is a way to see these new tools so that they may help draw renewed attention to God's

7. Newman, "Shocking Statistics."
8. Those who have been raised in the internet age.

goodness as revealed in the Bible. New models of learning and broader engagement with diverse, yet trusted voices, will be important. This offers us a new space of convergence where the past (trusted theological voices), the present (learning in the trenches), and future possibilities (leading on the front lines) must come together.

As a dad, I am learning that raising kids involves the courage to hear their new questions. That includes ideas about identity, global responsibility, ecological fears, the moral fabric of relationships, and the place of religion and spirituality. Sooner or later the Bible and its place in our lives must be an anchor we return to as we navigate such issues. Unfortunately, many have stopped trying to understand how to even wrestle with the diverse biblical truths alongside the next generation of digital natives. That means our homes, and sometimes even our churches, are not seen as safe places for those growing in a secular age who need to express doubts and disappointments.

An ancient biblical prayer recalls, "For [God] issued his laws to Jacob; he gave his instructions to Israel. He commanded our ancestors to teach them to their children, so the next generation might know them . . . so each generation should set its hope anew on God."[9] We cannot miss that as we revisit the promises recorded in the Bible, we want others to also put their trust in God. A fresh re-engagement with the Bible is about how we might help the next generation, gripped by shifts of a secular age, grow in hopefulness.

To reimagine the Bible requires that we pay special attention to how we read, teach, and speak about the Bible. The convergence of both secular assumptions and a digital revolution is new territory for us. The Slave Bible, and stories like it, point to a troubling paradox that will fuel the confusion already fermenting in our present contexts. To this we can add selfish agendas that build on private interpretations that lead people away from hearing the Bible as a living word from a loving God through a learning church community.

My hope is that as you read on, you will notice how easily we dismiss the world as completely evil and on a path to destruction. Instead, the Bible calls us to something more restorative. Although the Bible warns about "the ways of this world" and their destructive nature, it also promises God's gracious empowerment to be in the world but not of it. We are most worldly when we respond to "worldly" mockery with immaturity. My prayer is that

---

9. Ps 78:5–7 (NLT).

Introduction

we will return to the biblical promises that even the worst things we may experience cannot fully hinder or destroy the good things God is accomplishing.[10] We need a new perspective to see what is emerging. The late Andrew Walls once remarked, "The fundamental missionary experience . . . is to live on the terms set by someone else."[11] While you might not have signed up to be a missionary, a secular culture has imposed this new calling on every single Christian and this will include grappling with ideas being determined by our changing culture.

In our long history as Christians, the meaning of the Bible and its authority has involved deep and difficult conversations. Our present reality is no different, although the misuses, mockery, and misunderstandings at the heart of our secular age are new. As we explore, we will see that these new complexities of our secular age have not silenced our deep human need to hear essential truths about who we are, why we are here, and why that matters. I have sat with countless people looking for a safe place to share genuine questions and concerns as they notice the incongruities of their life and the discouraging issues in our world. These sacred moments have only confirmed that a secular culture cannot suppress how God has wired us to look for the truth, no matter how painful it is to hear.

ABOUT THE WORD "SECULAR"

The words *Bible* and *secular* might initially strike one as incompatible. I am guessing that these are not words or ideas you often associate with one another. Think about it. For most people, you either read the Bible, or you have bought into the values of a secular world. Part of the reason for this is that the bombardment of stories, in and out of the church, that capitalize on framing every disagreement as a battle between good and evil. What often follows is the pressure to choose, to know, to make up your mind and get on the winning side before it is too late.

Perhaps it is more natural, to think about life and its challenges as living in a messy middle, a paradox of sorts. This is in fact a reassuring biblical truth. Paul writes: "I do not understand what I do. For what I want to do I do not do, but what I hate, I do. And I do what I do not want to do."[12] Real life constantly requires discernment to revisit assumptions, correct blind

---

10. "He will complete the good work he started" (Phil 1:6).
11. Walls, *Missionary Movements*, 23.
12. Rom 7:15.

spots, and admit our weaknesses and sinful tendencies as we rethink habits to cultivate new ways to approach a changing world.

As we will see in Part 1 of this book, extreme separation between the Bible and secular culture blinds us to how the Bible reveals a God who brings divided things back together. Consider this: the New Testament books are written in Greek. If the earliest followers of Jesus, and later Christian communities, opted for a purely separationist approach, they would have *only* written the teachings of Jesus in Hebrew or Aramaic. This would have only furthered a division that was common in that ancient culture. Instead, and thankfully for us, they discerned that changing times required that they translate the Jewish sayings of Jesus for a Greek culture.

Two things that some would think could never be brought together were now converging. The Bible itself is a living reminder of God's vision to restore even linguistic division brought about by human sin.

I can just hear the argument now. "Who cares about the Greek culture? We need to hold on to the *true* Jesus who spoke Aramaic. Non-Jews need to learn our culture, our language, to understand him. That's the meaning of picking up your cross. Right?" Wrong! You and I are blessed by the fact that the story of Jesus and the gift of the Bible have been passed on, from their earliest records, as the living words for every generation to hear and understand. Over-reactions claiming a *pure* link over and against the Greek changing culture required discernment. Further, this should remind us that being counterculture is not the same as being anti-culture. This is foundational to understanding the rich gift of our Bible. The reason for this is that the Bible is meant to point to the living Word of Jesus that meets, confronts, corrects, and transforms *every* culture, including our own. Think about it. The Bible, in its New Testament portion, is in a language that Jesus and his earliest followers probably did not speak, at least not fluently.

I live in a multi-lingual context where debates about language occur daily. Without boring you with the politics of it all, trust me, it's complicated. Similar struggles were likely part of the journey that gave us our Bible. God's leading, Jesus' teaching, and the Holy Spirit's inspiriting all came together as those earliest followers of Jesus led in changing times. For too long, we have let a magical view that the Bible fell from the sky blind us to the sacrifices, struggles, and ongoing faithful guidance of the Holy Spirit that gave us the Bible.

A secular age has its own type of *cultural language*—values, ideals, and assumptions that we must consistently revisit with wisdom. This will require that we "translate," reaffirm, and repeat with gentleness truths found in the Bible as we grapple with a new language associated with our secular age. This new "language" encompasses habits and patterns that are still emerging. However, I believe there are notable signs pointing to new curiosity for spiritual truth, faith questions, and justice issues as people search for what it means to live a life of significance in a world of relational isolation and fragmentation.

Sarah Wilken Laflamme, a leading sociologist, notes that among groups of non-believers surveyed, "mystery" remains a category that captures what they believe. She writes: "The mystery worldview that we are all part of a mysterious and connected natural world and universe is the most popular non-belief worldview among Canadians who responded [to a survey]."[13] These revealing facts are good news as we consider our focus on the Bible. They point to fresh opportunities to discuss themes related to mystery and wonder and our need to know how to respond to the many unknowns of life.

By now, you may sense that I am proposing a posture toward this secular age that will likely not be reciprocated by those fully cemented in our secular culture. There will be moments when a biblical approach, even when shared respectably, will be ridiculed and resisted. Jesus' wisdom for us is to consider others and remain humble rather than use the ways of the world to address those influenced by the world. Here Jesus' way of peace and grace are to be made visible.[14] Consequently, my encouragement is to heed the biblical wisdom that says, "A soft or gentle answer turns away wrath, but a harsh word stirs up anger."[15]

THE SHAPE OF THIS BOOK

The word *secular* is not easy to define. As we'll soon see, it will take some time to understand it better. One scholar has highlighted the challenge of even just defining the term.[16] Aware of such challenges, Part 1 of this book will explore three phrases to guide us in understanding some of the complex realities that are defining this shifting secular age.

---

13. Laflamme, "Religion, Non-Belief, Spirituality," 14.
14. Phil 2:3–4.
15. Prov 15:1.
16. Hanson, "Secularization Thesis."

The Bible for a *Shifting* Secular Age

PART 1

THREE HANDLES: MAKING SENSE OF SOME SHIFTS IN THIS SECULAR AGE

I PASTOR IN ONE of the most "secular" places in North America. The City of Montreal, and the greater Montreal region, remains a leadership lab for learning about the challenges of our secular age. It is filled with lessons which include the pain related to misuses of the Bible and new, budding opportunities for re-imagining evangelism. About ten years ago we planted a church here knowing that there is no substitute for the proximity of journeying with those asking new, emerging questions. I am convinced that a biblical understanding of discipleship requires presence and personal connection. Moreover, this has helped us to see that "secular" is not just an academic idea, it's a practical reality in and among people we know and love, even if they are not sure what they believe about God.

A hallmark of our present culture is its resistance to clean definitions. To help with that we use the prefix *post*, as in postmodern, postcolonial, and post-reformation, to envision what may come "after" this season of turbulent change. It is my hope that the three phrases in Part 1 will provide memorable markers to help you lead and learn.

Less Religion, More Spirituality

From palm reading at a pool party, to strange funeral experiences, spirituality is in the air. The resurgence of astrology and interest in celestial signs and the paranormal is revealing a secular surprise we did not see coming. For the past few years, we have seen how the secular age emerging is more open to spirituality than anyone could have anticipated. Less religion and more spirituality is the handle that can help us get serious about this shift. What we will explore is the natural resistance toward religion yet a new longing for spiritual conversations and connectivity. As we consider why religion has gotten such a bad rap we will have to reconsider how we speak about the Bible. As part of this first chapter I will provide some thoughts to grapple with this growing shift.

Introduction

Less Power, More Participation

A growing spiritual curiosity includes a deep sense that we can all connect with God or gods on our own terms. For many, this helps bypass religion, which is equated with abuses of power. Moreover, a rejection of religion involves a renewed sense of self-guided participation. People desire to have life-changing encounters where one can participate in new experiences unhindered by tradition, and, at times, oppressive religious approaches. This is a growing hallmark of the current age. From peaceful protests to digital connectivity where one's authentic voice is heard, our secular age will be relentless at calling out misuses of power that silence participation. The Bible has so much to say about this. As we explore these tensions, we will have to reclaim a deeper way to talk about these issues since Jesus did promise a certain type of power, which requires that we all grapple with his unique *authority*.

Less Telling, More Teaching

Taylor Swift nailed it when at a commencement speech she said: "I won't tell you what to do because no one likes that. I will, however, give you some life hacks."[17] I think we are wise to consider how this secular age is shaped by a distrust in condescending methods of communication. Those in a secular age often associate this with church and unhealthy uses of the Bible focusing on telling people and trying to control what they do. If we are going to get a handle on the shifts of this secular age, we must consider moving away from domineering uses of the Bible that just tell people what to do. Instead, I want to suggest that this is a great time to re-engage with new modes of teaching that make room to explore mutual learning. The Bible offers wisdom for how to engage with those who doubt and distrust inauthentic voices. In light of many spiritual options, it is paramount that we consider how to move from telling to teaching and remember that the Bible provides numerous examples to guide us forward.

---

17. Taylor Swift, NYU Commencement Speech, 2022.

PART 2

THE BIBLE HEARD AS LIVING WORDS

Part 2 will keep in mind the above issues while exploring three images that celebrate the living nature of the words found in the Bible. I believe this approach can help us get past the barriers created by our secular culture. Further, the Bible calls us to respect those who doubt and struggle while exploring new, creative possibilities to help them understand the living nature of the Bible. Hearing the Bible as living words of truth has never been so important for reaffirming that it is a living God who speaks through the Bible. I have learned that this speaks to people's deepest human longings, which includes our need to hear the truth even if it is painful. No one wants a doctor who lies or a mechanic who tells half-truths. While a secular age shows resistances to universal truth claims, there are signs that living truth shared from authentic relationships and trusted communities is still possible and even desired by those in a secular age.

The Bible: Less of a Manual, More like a Compass

The Bible, because it is God's words for us, always points to life-giving truths that address the deepest parts of our humanity. Those in the secular age will need help to hear and understand the Bible in a way that makes sense to them. This chapter will explore the weakness of thinking of the Bible as an easy "fix-it" manual and the problematic outcomes this can cause. As a corrective, I explore how hear the Bible as living words that operate as a compass that reveals an awareness of our need to have purpose, to risk, to dream, and to step into new things God has in store for us. A compass provides direction without dictating every step—and this is exactly what is needed in times of change.

The Bible: Less of a Textbook, More like a Treasure

Digital natives and those shaped by a secular age can easily fall into a trap thinking religious books are just like boring textbooks. This is common and requires our attention in a way that speaks to the misuses and incorrect assumptions about the Bible. I want to revisit the importance of how we speak and teach about the Bible that highlights that it is a treasure that

Introduction

keeps providing new and shocking truth as we step into new seasons of life. Here we will explore and celebrate the rich resources that are timeless wisdom at the heart of the Bible.

The Bible: Fewer Rules, More Guidance for Restoring Relationships

The great North African theologian St. Augustine remarked that when we hear the Bible as living words we are transformed in a way that restores our relationships. He said, "Whoever thinks he has understood the divine scriptures or any part of them in such a way that his understanding does not build up the twin love of God and neighbor has not yet understood them at all."[18] For many in a secular culture, the Bible remains an ancient book of rules. This incorrect view of the Bible leads many to miss out on the living words in the Bible meant to cultivate healthy relationships. A secular age is clearly an age of fragmented relationships that rules alone cannot restore. While the Bible has commands for us, they are to be heard in the context of restoring relationships that keep us focused on a God who himself is a relational being.

WE HAVE DONE THIS BEFORE

During the sixteenth century, another time of chaotic change, God guided his people to face change by providing renewed attention on the special role of the Bible. The Reformation period, as it is now called, also saw the need to recenter and reimagine the gift of the Bible for an emerging world. The short memorable Latin phrases we still use are helpful handles. *Sola scriptura* or *sola fide* are just two of the most popular ones meant to be memorable yet indicative of a larger debate. While my phrases do not carry the gravitas of those left by the Reformation, they just might be memorable enough to guide us as we grapple with how to think about the Bible in this shifting secular age. While we may not be ready for a new Reformation, surely a Renaissance is needed.

As I write, I want to share from a place of deep blessing. For the past few years, I have seen women and men unlearn, rethink, and be stretched in the trenches of a secular age. Their faith and maturity have reaffirmed for me that the church, in all of its shortcomings, will continue to survive

---

18. Augustine, *On Christian Teaching*, 1:86.

when our hearts and minds remain attuned to the living words of God found in the Bible. The Holy Spirit is not a history teacher just reminding us of the good things in the past. Because he is God, he continues to inspire us to hear the written words anew. When this takes root, a new sense of joy to read the Scriptures becomes our new reality. There is no substitute for hearing and reading the Bible and having one's life anchored to God's larger plan of redemption. With this comes a surprising realization that the fear we feel is temporary in light of a lasting assurance that all authority in heaven and on earth remains firmly in the hands of Jesus, the eternal Word of God.

I recently met with some Christian leaders trying to understand the shifts they are seeing in their communities. As always, the Bible and our love for it came up. Soon, the discussion got heated as one person was adamant that we prepare for a battle. Raising their voice, they stated: "The Bible is the Word of God and it's offensive. People better get over it." While I could feel the passion related to their love for the Bible, I gently suggested that we think more carefully about what is happening. While the Bible causes a prideful heart to be humbled, we might want to reconsider that this shifting secular age is revealing a new generation who do not know or care enough about the Bible to even be offended.

The room got quiet, and the five-second pause felt like ten minutes. It soon hit me that indifference toward the Bible will be more challenging than the atheistic anger we anticipated.

Reading on will help you get serious about the Bible while facing the surprises of an emerging secular age, knowing that God's living ways, heard in his living words, is just what we need for what awaits us.

PART 1

Handles for Navigating the Shifts of a Secular Age

CHAPTER 1

Less Religion, More Spirituality

> "[B]elief versus disbelief, religion versus secularism . . . provide maps that are much neater and tidier than the spaces in which we find ourselves."
> –James K. A. Smith

GHOSTBUSTER AND SPIRITUAL SURPRISES

"Hi, Father, I need your help!" Those were the first words I heard as I opened our front door. Our neighbor, ignoring my explanation as to why people do not call me "Father," blurted: "Do you sprinkle oil on houses, like . . . um . . . a prayer against bad spirits?" With a pause she explained that a family member recently passed away and she thought that their spirit, like a ghost, could bring bad energy to her family due to an unresolved conflict. As if in a scene out of a *Ghostbuster* movie, she assumed a priest could help. She figured an oil sprinkling with a prayer might do the trick. After calming her concerns, I reassured her that there were other options to navigate the grief and her fear of evil spirits.

Some may dismiss such stories as silly, but I want to suggest that they may be pointing to an emerging sign for understanding our culture as well as the Bible better. Our present secular age is revealing a surprising openness to spiritual matters as a way of exploring one's interior life. Hearing this will be paramount if we hope to see people read and better understand the biblical wisdom that addresses spiritual matters. Throughout this book I will highlight how this resurgence in spirituality also includes questions about faith, God, the Bible, and the way to make sense of fragmented relationships and suffering. More importantly, I believe these issues point to our human yearning to discover the life we are meant to live.

As I have shared stories like the one above, I am no longer surprised when leaders, parents, and pastors respond with similar examples. A pattern in many of these conversations is that people have "less interest in religion and more curiosity around spirituality." This is surely not the secular world we expected. The late Peter Berger, a leading sociologist, noted a possible resurgence in these matters. He once stated, "Let me, then, repeat what I said a while back, the world today is . . . anything but the secularized world that had been predicted . . . by so many analysts of modernity."[1] Our old definitions of "secular" are being rewritten and this will have huge implications for leadership, faith, church, and how people think and engage with the Bible.

In this first chapter, I will suggest that one shift of this secular culture is a brisk and growing interest in diverse forms of spirituality. It should concern us that this comes at a time when reading and understanding the Bible is at an all-time low. Consider that a 2022 report revealed drastic decline in Bible engagement. With particular focus on the impact of COVID, researchers observed how Bible reading saw "the steepest, sharpest decline on record."[2] Spiritual promptings can be subjective and difficult to discern. For this reason, it should come as a wake-up call to hear of this new spiritual curiosity as we deal with a decline in biblical learning. In fact, it is time to admit that while the Bible remains the world's best-selling book, fewer and fewer people are reading it.[3] [4]

Time magazine recently highlighted a growing interest in spiritual matters among young people. This was linked to the discovery and use of astrology apps, suggesting that Gen Zers are turning into "believers."[5] Polling organizations like Alpha and Barna point to research revealing an openness to new spiritual questions. All this left pollsters describing the next generation as the "Open Generation."[6] If that is not enough, Springtide

---

1. Berger, ed., *Desecularization of the World*, 9.
2. Macinnis, "Report: 26 Million Americans Stopped Reading the Bible," lines 17–18.
3. Radosh, "Good Book Business."
4. Or even learning to read it properly.
5. Bruner, "High-Tech Astrology Apps."
6. Barna Group, "Open Generation."

Research Institute observes similar trends in their document *The State of Religion and Young People: Exploring the Sacred*.[7]

All these point to a shift in our secular age that will require a robust and healthy re-engagement with the Bible to discern and confront aspects related to new spiritualities. Older approaches for defining a secular age miss the possibilities, and at times, optimism around faith, God, and spirituality. In fact, older definitions of our secular age often dismiss these shifts as dangerous without pausing to consider the human dynamic they reveal. It is my hope that leaders who care about the Bible will reconsider how these shifts may provide new spaces to explore doubts as people discern what a living God might have to say about all this. I believe we are living at the cusp of a ripe season for affirming and celebrating the special role of the Bible and the wisdom it provides about the joy of spiritual life rooted in the love of God. All this is possible if we readjust our perspective about what we once believed about the secular age.

LESS RELIGION AND THE ISSUE OF GRIEF

In 1888, when Mark Twain visited Montreal, he recalled it as "a city where you couldn't throw a brick without breaking a church window."[8] Those days are long gone and many are still living through the realities of such change. Before we address what more spirituality might entail, I want to suggest that less religion breeds its own type of loss. For some, stats related to church closures or declining church attendance pinpoint the sadness.[9] However, more lies beneath the surface. Change is hard but change linked to the loss of what we associate with God and his loving presence can be very challenging. I have noticed that grief, when not addressed well, makes us vulnerable to certain temptations that ignore new opportunities. Three temptations that I have consistently seen require our attention if we hope to wisely navigate the shifts of this present secular age.

Temptation to Lean toward Confrontation

"Less religion" can feel like a loss of identity. For many, this is linked to our cultural addiction to polarizing discourses. As a leader, a husband, and a

---

7. Springtide Research Institute, *State of Religion and Young People 2023*.
8. CBC Arts, "Montreal's Historic Reputation," lines 1–3.
9. Pew Research Center, "Decline of Christianity."

father, I am trying to model a nuanced way of thinking that I know my kids and future generations will need to develop well. It remains a shock to some that God can guide us to be both people of conviction and people who are respectful and nuanced in those convictions. This involves better listening, less rushing to conclusions, and heeding the biblical command that includes being slow to speak. Loud voices and media narratives often convince us that less religion is about *anti-religion*. This, again, is often the way an older narrative of a secular culture framed this loss. However, less interest in religion and church is not always indicative of people who want to attack all religious ideas.

The storm we find ourselves in equates our feelings of loss with a justified posture of confrontation. Without realizing it we let our reactions toward the culture become dictated by the values of the worst of this secular agenda. I have seen some who call themselves Bible-believing Christians act just like those who have never opened a Bible in their lives. Soon, many start to see every life issue through the filter of winners and losers. Here our secular age blinds us to the rich and more humane biblical way that reminds us that we are all lost, and God has a way to meet us in our mess. When the Bible no longer shapes how we listen and engage, an attitude of confrontation is inevitable. It is time to admit that "win" and "lose" categories do not do justice to the hopeful promises found in the Bible, which portray God as one who has come to seek and save us.

As I noted in the Introduction, I pastor in a shifting secular context. Here confrontation has already been substituted for indifference. Our staff often hears me say: "People in a secular culture do not care enough about us to argue with us." Nevertheless, I think something painful is taking place in the church. It involves our deep struggle to deal with loss and to learn from it. Whenever we feel we are losing influence, losing our place, losing our kids to a changing world, we assume a confrontational way is the best way to defend what we love. This sense of loss fuels our fears, making it hard to grow, mature, and adapt to what is happening. All of this can easily coalesce into diverse *feelings* that minimize the need to think and listen to what is taking place in this *emerging* secular culture.

TEMPTATION TO LEAN TOWARD CONFORMING

In contrast, the other extreme can be described as a posture of *conforming*. In fact, those who believe that confrontation is necessary point to people who conform as examples of weakness. Influenced by a secular culture, we are invited to conform and just go with the flow. Further, those who conform to the pressures may be tempted to define "to conform" as being more loving. I have heard some argue: "Well, Jesus didn't fight, so neither should we." While this seems noble, just like a confrontational outlook, "conforming" minimizes the new ways that God might be at work that do not always fit into either perspective.

This temptation, as with a confrontational approach, often uses the Bible to justify these deep feelings of loss. When confrontational or conforming approaches take root, they become a dominant lens for how we *use* and *interpret* the Bible. Preaching that fuels these feelings makes it hard to hear the biblical wisdom that God has always equipped and empowered his people in times of change. Now, don't get me wrong, there are times when we must respond with strong resistance or thoughtful adjustment; yet we will need patience and wisdom rooted in a deeper understanding of the Bible to discern when that is.

TEMPTATION TO QUIT

A few months ago, I met with an older leader in our church who displayed signs of the loss described above. Now a grandparent, they spoke about all the changes and how disorienting it is even in a church that they love. As a newer church trying to engage in a secular age, my own church feels this tension related to loss. Perhaps you have had similar conversations. I want to encourage you that there is a way forward in this new secular age if we can get honest about how we process loss. To many people, "less religion" means loss of control. If not careful, they will interpret that loss by quitting and washing their hands of it all. As I listened to that leader in our church, I reminded them that we will need the wisdom and examples of young and old to navigate change, all while we all trust in God. This will be a gift to a new generation. In fact, I have often sat and watched the slow disappearance of spiritual grandparents, noting how a secular culture can deprive us of much needed wisdom if we fail to help people not fall for the temptation to quit. This too is part of the Bible's prayerful insights that is at the root of a biblical prayer that reads: "We're not keeping this to ourselves, we're passing it along to the next generation—God's fame and fortune, the marvelous things he has done."[10]

10. Ps 73:4 (Message).

One helpful way to move beyond loss is related to a biblical outlook that reminds us that God, in the power of the Holy Spirit, is at work in his people, who are called to live with the biblical promise that God *still* transforms culture.[11] This outlook has helped me lead in a secular context and protect myself from the temptation to overreact when facing unforeseen shifts. Leadership in a secular age will require a deep awareness of this in ourselves and those we lead. While my context in Montreal may vary from your context, the things we are seeing have clearly extended beyond our context and the shifts of a secular culture continue to expand. We can learn and lead, or we can forfeit our place, worry and quit. Even large churches that were once signposts of health and growth are no longer engaging the current generation in meaningful and consistent ways. Navigating this loss for families and grandparents requires wisdom that can position us to deal with the shifts that await.

The shifts that this book will address will require new tools, categories, and ideas to grapple with a secular age that wants less religion and more spirituality. When I was younger, I was drawn to a church that only gave me one approach to the Bible, one that aggravated my loss with anger. The preacher regularly framed the changes in the world by capitalizing on the feelings of loss. With that came an outlook suggesting everything in the world was "right vs. wrong," "good vs. bad," "me vs. you." It took some time to notice that I was also reading the Bible through that lens. It took time to grow out of that perspective to learn that not *all* things fit a binary and somewhat simplistic approach. Most troubling was that this polarizing approach made it hard to celebrate the good things God was doing and how the Bible could guide me even when I wasn't always sure what to do or how to respond.

WHAT IS "MORE" SPIRITUALITY?

In this secular age, words like "spiritual" or "spirituality" are often used interchangeably. They are often applied to diverse emotional encounters beyond our grasp. I think Rodney Clapp was on to something when he proposed that the term *spirituality* gained popular use "largely because it seems capacious, inclusive, non-dogmatic, and non-judgmental."[12]

---

11. Niebuhr, *Christ and Culture*. See also Thompson, *Christ and Culture in the New Testament*.

12. Clapp, *Tortured Wonders*, 233.

Less Religion, More Spirituality

Over the years, in classrooms, conferences, and even in churches, I have seen faces light up as people expressed their own desire for God, a sense of faith and what they described as spiritual moments. Some of these stories were linked to possible signs from God. For others, it was an answer to prayer during a season of grief. For some, it was about a longing that their lives were part of something bigger. Amid the diversity of stories, "spiritual" was used to speak of something meaningful, positive, with a deep human desire to know that one can connect with God.

The Bible offers an ancient prayer of reflection. It states: "What are mere mortals that you should think about them, human beings that you should care for them."[13] I think of this as an honest confession that points to our human feelings related to *spirituality*. In our secular age, when I hear people use the word *spiritual*, I think of these words as I recall that God has created us for intimate connection and that this living God cares about us by drawing attention to our frailty.

Our shifting secular age can blur important biblical truth and distort our perspective so that we forget God's caring ways. Although we are "mere humans," we are still created with an extraordinary longing for spiritual awareness. This includes a desire for meaning and mystery that find their coherence in God's goodness. While we can never find our way to God, we are constantly aware that we are lost if he doesn't find us. If we can guide people to see their longing for *more spirituality* as a yearning rooted in an internal dimension of our shared humanity and our God-given nature, I think we can help people connect the dots and understand how the Bible addresses our deepest spiritual questions.

Questions like "do we all have a guardian angel?" or "what's the best way to connect with people we love who are dead?" pop up regularly as I share with people that I am a spiritual leader who teaches about God and the Bible. As we have noted, this is not the secular context we anticipated, yet these conversations point to the ease with which people share their experiences and questions when they feel safe or heard. Less religion and more spirituality may be a simple handle, yet it can be a helpful starting point for how we might go deeper as issues continue to shift. This must include rethinking what we once believed about a secular culture. For years, I heard the word *secular* used to mean "anti-Christian" or "anti-God" and even "atheistic." But things are shifting. Can we move past old categories

---

13. Ps 8:4 (NLT).

and consider that the shifts upon us are much too complex to fit into such a simplistic paradigm?

WHEN SECULAR AND SPIRITUAL COLLIDE

For the rest of this chapter, I want to explore three opportunities and some unforeseen challenges that await the shift to less religion and more spirituality. One has to do with the growing influence of a digital culture that easily stirs curiosity in the paranormal, aliens, death, astrology, and what lies beyond the material world alone. Another opportunity involves dispelling the myth that "secular" is somewhere "out there." Old assumptions are fading and even people who embrace a faith tradition must think about the way a secular age is changing them as well. Lastly, the Bible helps with this if we revisit and reclaim a biblical category that has gotten lost, the God-fearer.

In 2023, Joe Rogan interviewed two popular young ghost hunters and paranormal explorers.[14] While Rogan is an enigmatic and at time polarizing figure, his guests often include scientists, medical practitioners, fitness specialists, and cultural personalities. In his interview with teenage paranormal guys, the discussion became more fascinating as they acknowledged the possibility of the dead being able to communicate with the living and the excitement of finding haunted places inhabited by spirits.

When I mentioned the names of these modern-day "ghostbusters" to my kids, they quickly knew who they were. They then told me of their other online videos, which have millions of views. It is this digital tsunami that reveals we must move past old "faith against science" debates and acknowledge a collision between the spiritual and the secular, and watch for the overlap as new spaces for unexpected conversations emerge. These will include discussions about faith, spirituality, wellness, inner healing, psychology, and much more. This is great news for those of us who care about our friends and family, who may not know that the Bible addresses many of these themes. The endless possibilities for conversations and new questions will be key for rethinking what we say and how God is at work in ways we never expected.

These new spiritual spaces will require us to listen without overreacting. I have numerous examples of feeling unsure myself when strange questions push toward the bizarre paranormal, the psychedelic, and esoteric

---

14. *The Joe Rogan Experience*, Episode 1922: Sam and Colby.

rituals. The Bible has warnings as well as regular reminders about how God's presence casts out fear. This is a promise we need to hold on to as we see the growing reconnection with astrology apps, goddess cards, and online tarot games, even as the spiritual ways of Jesus found in the Bible are ignored or misunderstood.[15]

This is a great time to consider how we might reclaim the importance of the Bible, but it will take time to regain a healthy perspective that displays and fosters trust. I recently got invited to an online livestream class on how to spot demons and experience spiritual deliverance. Dreadfully, it came from a person I know who rarely attends church and has inadequate theological training, yet has amassed numerous followers online. After hearing a few comments, I noticed how random Bible stories were all mixed together without any concern for theological accuracy or coherence. While frustrated at that way new digital tools can lead to confusion, I was also aware of this new hunger people have for understanding the interior, spiritual dimensions of life, including healing that often falls in the category of deliverance.

Years ago, the term *religious nones* was invented as an attempt to frame what was happening. It refers to those who, when asked about their beliefs, say they have "none" that align with a particular religion. Here less religion goes as far as no religion. Subsequently, the research on the next generation also states, "Although many *nones* are nonbelievers or agnostic . . . they are also those who hold beliefs in a higher power."[16] Connecting with this higher power is another way of expressing one's own spiritual interests.

As we've also noted, researchers at Barna[17] have described the youngest generation as the Open Generation.[18] If you recall, this coincides with some of the important evangelistic work being doing among leaders in the Alpha organization. This new and unexpected openness means many things that will open room to dialogue about faith, God, suffering, spirituality, Jesus, and how the Bible may have important things to teach us in this regard. In addition, research on mental health in young people and

---

15. In one BBC study, research reveals a boom in astrology apps for our anxious age: see Parkin, "Anxieties and Apps."

16. Thiessen and Laflamme, *None of the Above*, 4.

17. The Barna Group is a reliable firm studying trends and statistics related to church and cultural engagement.

18. Barna Group, "Open Generation."

their struggle to make sense of new forms of isolation also find a link with a return to spiritual curiosity.[19]

Less religion and more spirituality has never been truer for how we think about emerging secular spaces and people's conflicted and curious views on death. I regularly find myself with those who reveal their views of spirituality in moments of deep grief. Recently, I found myself at a funeral for someone I didn't really know. The family was struggling to say goodbye due to a sad death during the pandemic. Through a connection with someone in our church they asked if I could help. After praying, I sensed it was a good opportunity to model care, hope, and learning from the kinds of "spiritual" conversations that might emerge. As I have learned, grief almost always includes spiritual openness.

Before I got up to say some closing words, family members went to the mic to share their own stories of the deceased. These included still hearing the deceased talk with them. Quickly my hyper-spiritual meter went to a whole new level. Almost every person who spoke at the mic suggested *the spirit* of person who had passed away was still in the room with us at the funeral home. One even claimed they could sense the dead person in the room looking down on us. Maybe I missed that class in seminary, but few will be ready for the new secular realities revealing a new world that is less religious and more spiritual and more detached from an understanding of the Bible that can help us discern what is healthy and what is not.

Although a bigger picture is still emerging, one other outcome of this collision of secular and spiritual involves a growing health and wellness movement. Alternative medicine, natural food, and other wellness products are framed in spiritual terms. While there is nothing wrong with a day of rest at the spa, the endless tools for self-fulfilling spiritual seekers coupled with wellness feel-good tips is now a trillion-dollar industry.[20] One day, while teaching his closest followers, Jesus, assuming they knew what was happening at street level in their communities, asked: "Hey, what are people saying about me? Your peers, your family members, what's the word on the street? What are people saying as they think about the spiritual issues I'm addressing?"[21]

If Jesus were to ask us a similar question today, we would have to say that people are tired and exhausted with fighting about religion. In the

---

19. Springtide Research Institute, "Gen Z and Religion."
20. Callaghan et al., "Feeling Good."
21. Matt 16:13–20, paraphrased.

same breath, we would likely add that there seems to be a growing interest in matters of spiritual exploration and a hunger to find a meaningful place to contribute to a changing world. We are all looking for a way to make sense of the life we were meant to live. Maybe you noticed that Jesus doesn't say: "What do religious teachers at the temple think?" Instead, there is a grassroots vibe in the question—"The people you hang with, those on the street, what are they thinking?" Perhaps it was his way of saying, "While old narratives remain evident, what new things do you hear from those closest to you?"

Phil Zuckerman, in his *Living the Secular Life,* may offer a first step into hearing what those in secular spaces still long for. He writes: "A lack of belief in God does not render this world any less wondrous, lush, mystifying, or amazing."[22] It seems Zuckerman has put his finger on a core issue. If secular culture is truly shaping up to be less religious and more inquisitive and curious about spiritual matters, it will also be just as open to questions about beauty, love, joy, and hope. This is good news, since the Bible and the rich legacy of the Christian story have much to say about these kinds of issues. Since Part 2 of this book will explore this in depth, I simply recall here the biblical truth that God "has also set eternity in the human heart..."[23]

SECULAR AND THE MYTH OF "OUT THERE"

A few years ago, I was a speaker at a Christian camp. I had an interaction that reminded me of a common hurdle we must address if we hope to speak with clarity to those in this shifting secular culture. In the distance, a parent called out: "Pastor, we are so happy you are our camp speaker this week." After I responded with a quick "thank you," the dear mom asked, "Can you pray for me? My son is struggling with issues in school, and he is doubting his faith with all this 'secular' stuff." It was a deep, honest moment. After a prayer, I realized more was needed since prayer is God's gift to surrender, act, and learn.

I proposed a longer chat to grapple with her comments about this "secular" stuff. As we are doing in this book, I wanted to provide a different perspective that might alleviate her fears. As it is so common, "secular" for many does not include spirituality and our human search for longing and wholeness. Instead, the word *secular* is used geographically as something

---

22. Zuckerman, *Living the Secular Life,* 212.
23. Eccl 3:11.

"out there" in the world, removed from what we consider safe: church, youth group, Christian camp, Christian school, etc. Now I think these are important places that should be safe, but they do not provide a natural, invisible barrier to the way a secular age informs, shapes, and shifts how we think. Moreover, when secular is defined as something just "out there," it makes us view people who do not believe what we believe as those we must fix before they can join us "in here." The Bible does not present such a simplistic approach to the Christian life and our place in the world.

Imagine a finger pointing "out there." For many, that is where "secular" is. "In here," meaning church or camp, this, we might think, is holy, non-secular, Christian domain. We must correct this outlook if we are to get serious about reimagining the Bible that speaks to people who might having varying viewpoints about God and faith. The truth is that many secular values do not follow these clean lines of thinking we use to make sense of complexities. "Secular" involves a complex set of values, ideas, and assumptions that now includes spiritual realities. Although I understood that the mom at camp wanted to talk about the values that seemed contrary to the Bible, she had missed that "secular" is much more fluid than a place somewhere out in the world.

I want to suggest that all future conversations, if they are to be fruitful, will require that we rethink the way we use or understand the term *secular*. In so doing, we should be aware of how we *all* have been impacted, to some degree, by a secular view of life. Consider a secular vision of freedom. This involves our right to define and pursue a happy life as we see fit. This is a secular value, not necessarily a biblical value. While it is not a biblical idea, it is something we appreciate as a value of our secular world. The point is that secular is not always bad or good and it definitely not just something out there. Personal choice to do what one wants with their time, their body, their money is informed by a secular principle rooted in individualism, self-authenticity, and self-expression. This "secular" value is not just out there in the world, it informs those in and out of church, no matter what their beliefs are.

Imagine that for thousands of years people only defined themselves in relation to their place of birth. This meant that their identity was defined in reference to their father, owner, ruler, or clan. Jesus is often described as son of Mary, from a region called Nazareth. In the Bible, marriages were arranged, jobs were decided based on guild, and personal happiness was not a part of people's vocabulary. No one I know wants to revert to that approach to life; instead, we enjoy the freedoms that are an overflow of a modern world. We take for granted how comfortable we are with these types of secular values. We might even like and celebrate certain secular values that have to do with social changes, but we don't like "secular" when it involves religious issues. I am not sure we can so easily have one without the other.

Coming back to my family camp conversation, I remember how the space to process these types of ideas helped parents to understand that they needed to think more deeply if they were going to understand their kids and the world emerging around them. What I tried to suggest is something I hope we begin to understand at the outset of this book. The term *secular* is not just something out there beyond what you or I consider a safe place, with some bad agenda for the world. The secular involves a set of shifting values, habits, assumptions, and beliefs that, over time, can create space for either good or bad decisions. The earliest followers of Jesus we meet in the Bible had to learn to engage with their changing culture just as we will have to with ours.

For many years, we have been beating a drum that presented secular culture as something that would be anti-God, anti-Bible, anti-Christ. In some radical examples this may be the case, but what is also happening is a most unexpected turn. A leading theologian was spot on when he said: "If I say that this is a post-Christian nation, that doesn't mean necessarily non-Christian."[24] We are wise to remember that a growing number of people fully shaped by a secular culture are likely to be unfamiliar with Christianity more than against it. An overreaction to the term *secular,* always assuming a negative and godless view of life, may cause us to miss an important biblical category that can help us re-engage people who are longing for more than this life has to offer.

RECLAIMING AN ESSENTIAL BIBLICAL CATEGORY: GOD-FEARER

Throughout the New Testament we meet non-Jews who were respected and encouraged in their search for God. The biblical term is often translated "God-fearer." They were not unbelievers and not Jewish, but something in between. For example, consider Lydia. Part of her story is found in Acts 16. We know she was a businesswoman who was likely well off. As part of a common cultural practice, she made her way to pray outside the city with

---

24. Sparrow, "Britain is now 'Post-Christian,'" para. 4.

other spiritual types. The Bible calls her "a worshipper of God"[25] with no official religious affiliation. One day, to her surprise, Lydia meets some new people who had gathered to pray, and they connect her deep spiritual longings to Jesus' living ways. Subsequently, she wants to hear more. I will let you read on to see how her life is changed forever, but I want us to consider that the Bible provides other stories of those who were seeking to connect with God like this. This happened because all people look for ways to explore and understand the life they were meant to live. Fast-forward to today, and I think the term "spiritual seeker" may be synonymous with those the Bible called God-fearer. Although some mock the ongoing dialogue with those who do not believe, I propose we let the Bible guide us again.

A brief note for clarity: God-fearer is not the same as "fear of God." When the Bible uses the term "fear of God," it is often referring to how Israel should worship only the God of Israel. Hence, "fear of God" is meant to convey a posture of worship that those who are *already* believers should display. On the other hand, we meet in the New Testament diverse individuals who are exploring faith and spirituality. Due to the many religious options in the ancient world, the Bible describes certain spiritual seekers as "God-fearers." As noted above, they are not Jewish but they do show reverence and respect for all kinds of gods. In that way, a "God fearer" is a spiritual seeker curious and conscious of divine concerns but not yet a believer in just one God. For our present discussion I want to focus on "God-fearer" as a biblical category that provides invaluable insights for how to manage the possibilities of emerging secular realities where more spirituality than we once anticipated is becoming common.

Based on archaeological evidence, we know that "God-fearers" were Greeks who often explored faith with Jews. Some also donated funds to support a Jewish synagogue. They respected local Jewish communities as they found themselves welcome to explore and reflect on their desire to appease God even if they weren't always sure how to do that. These non-Jews remained rooted in their gentile identities, which meant they did not consider being circumcised so as to become full participants in the Jewish faith. One New Testament scholar goes as far as stating:

> Most pagans . . . affiliated with synagogue communities *as pagans*. This was a very long-lived and socially stable arrangement: from the Hellenistic period on through centuries after the accession of

---

25. Acts 16:14.

Constantine, synagogues continued to accommodate sympathetic outsiders.[26]

The term *pagan* here is not meant to be heard as negative. It was a common way to indicate non-Jews, including those known as Greek God-fearers who sensed they were welcome to see, support, and, in limited ways, participate within the Jewish religious framework.[27] This was also in line with an area of the temple called the gentile court, which allowed non-Jews to mingle, watch, listen, and at times participate with their own spiritual questions and prayerful concerns. Maybe you are starting to see the pattern. The Bible is such a gift to us as we consider what is happening in our time. Having been birthed in a pluralistic age, Christianity, from its inception, was able to adapt and adjust to diverse ways that spirituality was explored.

It has never been more important to reconsider that maybe our emerging secular context is pointing us to return to the Bible and to explore new spaces that will help us engage and encourage those in our secular age who are "God-curious" as they sense that old secular promises never materialized. I have come back to the idea of "God-fearers" often as we started a church. In fact, we wanted to make it safe for people to visit the church, hear the Bible, and engage in community as a "God-fearer," knowing that Jesus alone still moves people from curiosity to Christ-centered commitment. In fact, years ago *Christianity Today* referred to Quebec as "the Prodigal Province." It was good news, since God loves to welcome prodigals as they are while he lovingly reveals to them who they are meant to be.[28]

God-fearer remains a biblical category we are blessed to have as we work through the new secular spaces that include spirituality. As I reflect on my own journey, I think this category speaks to my earliest religious memories informed by my Roman Catholic upbringing. Born to immigrant parents, I remember that my upbringing left little room to ask questions about God or faith. As is common with immigrant families, we were to respect what our families passed on to us. Nevertheless, as a young teenager I began to question, even deconstruct, what I believed while remaining respectful to my family. As you consider your own journey, how would you describe those early questions about God, faith, and spirituality?

---

26. Fredricksen, "Who Was Paul?," 35 (emphasis mine).

27. Likely the Jewish sect known as Zealots would not have appreciated such connection.

28. Hovsepian, "Quebec: Canada's Prodigal Province."

In my life there was a crossroads kind of moment. It was a painful experience that involved a family member who was diagnosed with a rare blood infection. All the tears and prayers didn't keep her alive. This thrust me into my late teenage years with unexpected doubts about God and his love for me and my family. However, I still considered myself a "God-fearer" as some sympathetic people let me work out what I really believed and what I hoped God would do in my life. Although my Roman Catholic upbringing was positive, within a short time my family became acquainted with a Protestant church. As a young Christian, this felt like a different religion from my earlier Roman Catholic experience.

Just like secular "God-fearers," I was confused by intra-Christian denominations. As mentioned earlier, a family member who eventually turned to agnostic spirituality once remarked: "To those in a secular age Christianity comes across like a pluralistic religion." That has continued to haunt me since it rings so true to what I felt early on. If we let the Bible guide us, we will notice that those who define themselves as spiritual today are similar to the "God-fearers" of the Bible. Moreover, they model similar patterns for spiritual interest in the face of religious infighting, "buffet" or "cafeteria" spiritualities, and distrust toward oppressive religious authorities.

In my Canadian context, there is a historical period known as the Quiet Revolution; many in my generation were having their own personal quiet revolution.[29] We were quietly doubting, struggling, wondering, and searching, but found little room to express questions in church or with our family. As the exodus from church accelerated the old secular narratives took root. Few anticipated that Quebec's secular vision of the future was ripe for new revival of beliefs to emerge. Susan Palmer notes: "Quebec is a really good place if you are a new prophet, and you want to set up your religious organization . . . There is a kind of void that new religions rush into opportunistically."[30]

As we engage in this shifting secular age, I believe the biblical category of God-fearers remains most helpful. Just as with Lydia, similar stories are taking place all around us. Even as a wealthy businesswoman, Lydia found time to pray and connect with the local spiritual beliefs of her community.

---

29. The Quiet Revolution designates a period in the late 1960s related to a colossal shift in the role of religion in the province of Quebec. It was a time when the Roman Catholic Church was marginalized, relinquishing influence and power in numerous public spheres. With it, a new vision of religious neutrality emerged. For many, it was a significant marker for the emergence of a new vision of a secular society.

30. Mosimann, "Reconceptualizing High Power(s)," para. 4.

Less Religion, More Spirituality

As the Bible explains, God opened her mind to understand and respond to Paul's message, pointing to the good news only Jesus could give. She had money, but that wasn't enough for the life she was meant to live. Soon she was baptized and likely became one of the key leaders of the church plant that would take root in Philippi. Yes, she was a single, female, spiritually curious God-fearer—who revealed that even her wealth and influence were not enough to quench the deeper questions of life.

Future God-fearers are all around us, looking, searching, and yearning. They are tired of the lies and unfulfilled promises of a secular age. Infighting between Christians will only create more hurdles for those who are adamant that we need less religion. My goal in describing my context is to let you know that this is not just a Quebec phenomenon. In fact, in our present secular experience we will keep seeing an awakening that may be a harbinger of what is to come for other places in North America. While it may be tempting to fall for naïve or overly aggressive responses, I want to conclude by suggesting the need to create a new way forward.

SPIRITUAL FREEDOM AND CREATIVE POSSIBILITIES

Aware of the tensions described above, I propose that a way forward requires an imaginative vision that corrects the older definition of secular. Less religion and more spirituality will require a careful, yet essential, return to the biblical promise that God is with us until the end of any age. This truth will protect us from extremes while providing renewed strength to seek new paths to hear how God is still speaking to us through the Bible. As those dependent on the Holy Spirit, we know why spirituality matters to people. It is an aspect of being made in the image of a God who breathes life into us. Remember that we can celebrate spirituality as we suggest that there are healthy guidelines for a flourishing spiritual life rooted in the gospel.

The earliest followers of Jesus were in new territory as the early years of the church took root. The era we associate with the early church reveals the hard work they undertook to revisit and rearticulate what was familiar to them yet required reinterpretation for new God-fearers. Old categories were being reworked from a new center founded on Jesus' life, death, resurrection, and ascension. One of my professors termed this process a "hermeneutical conversion."[31] It is an awareness that a change of perspective is needed. It happens when one returns to a story, an idea, even a belief, and

---

31. A phrase used by the late Charles Kannengiesser.

begins to see it in a new way. This shift, when applied to the Bible, helps us consider what the earliest followers of Jesus went through. They had to revisit the Old Testament, which they knew well, considering Jesus' teaching. In this "conversion," they returned to the Old Testament to consider what they had missed considering the long-awaited Messiah now being fully revealed in Jesus.

This meant that all the followers of Jesus who were Jewish needed to have a conversion of the mind. They had to revisit the same biblical stories of the Old Testament they thought they knew and consider that Jesus' arrival was creating a new understanding for them. This collided with older categories as the resurrection birthed a new world without comparison. In some ways, my book is an invitation to return to the Bible and consider a new thing awaiting us in our shifting secular contexts. Can we believe that resurrection is still transforming even dead and discouraging things in our world? If so, can we imagine what the Bible can still guide us as we seek new ways to speak about Jesus and his love and discern what those in our secular culture need to hear to live the life they were meant to live?

May those we meet find us creating new bridges of connection that magnify the goodness of God and the love of Jesus. Some have called for the need of "third spaces" where we can listen as we create new ways to address what's happening.[32] This, I believe, may be exactly what our emerging secular culture is crying out for, as the burden of polarizing language reveals its dehumanizing limits. Where the Spirit of the Lord is there is freedom. This freedom must include freedom to ask, explore, and share one's questions that most likely involve diverse approaches to spirituality and less religion.

The field of neuroplasticity confirms that even after a horrible accident causing brain injury, people can recreate new points of connection. Dr. Mark Tuszynski notes that after a traumatic experience the brain needs "encouraging environments for regrowth."[33] Similarly, the traumatic shifts of our secular age will require new links for spiritual regrowth that make fresh connections with the Bible. When this happens, people who are wondering and longing for answers should meet people like you and me who

---

32. Conti, "Do Yourself a Favor." For most, the two dominant social spaces we inhabit are work and home, yet we need "third spaces" for a robust maturity, social interactions, and community engagement. Third spaces are in-between contexts, such as coffee shops, gyms, a music venue, and the church.

33. Science Daily, "Adult Brain Repairs Itself," para. 7.

love the Bible and who are safe to talk with and get honest about why spiritual matters still feel important even in a secular age.

The new connections that can lead to regrowth will entail uses of the Bible that create rather than cut. For too long, we have let cutting interpretations just highlight our disagreements. Those deeply entrenched in this secular age will capitalize on such shallow thinking and move further from the Bible, not closer. In fact, years ago Lesslie Newbigin observed how conflict causes us to lose sight of deeper issues. He wrote: "How will the world believe a message which we do not appear to believe ourselves?"[34] I am afraid to admit it, but until we create models of unity with other Christians those in a secular age will continually wonder about the sufficiency of the Bible and the gift it is meant to be. If we desire people to re-engage with the Scriptures, as we should, we can no longer ignore how a secular culture interprets our disagreement as an indication of the weakness of our message.

A few weeks into planting a church I was asked to sit on a panel of leaders from different religions. A local TV station had a segment on faith, God, and spiritual things and they invited the new guy in town. I'll never forget when the host began the conversation by stating: "I am spiritual but not religious," and then lobbed a first question my way, "How would you define spiritual?" All my years of theological studies had not prepared me for the shift I was experiencing on TV. I remember slowly piecing together different ideas, but to this day, I wish I would have provided a better response. I think my lack of clarity revealed how ill-prepared I was then for the surprises that this secular context was already producing. I hope that reading on helps you prepare for the new surprises coming our way.

---

34. Newbigin, *Is Christ Divided?*, 9. His focus was the sufficiency of the atonement and the related disagreements.

CHAPTER 2

Less Power, More Participation

"You will receive power."—Jesus

TAKE THE POWER BACK?

THICH QUANG DUC, IN the summer of 1963, was the center of global attention. Startlingly, he set himself on fire in broad daylight. It was an act of defiance against the abuses of power toward him and fellow Buddhist monks. The image of such a painful display of conviction led President Kennedy to assert: "No news picture in history has generated so much emotion around the world as that one."[1] I remember the picture as the cover art for an album by the band Rage Against the Machine, a popular group that fused poetic lyricism and catchy guitar riffs evoking justified rage against oppressive regimes. One of the popular tracks on that album was called "Take the Power Back." It seems as relevant today as when I first heard it years ago.

Any attempt to address the importance of the Bible today requires listening to the brewing frustration of those who, in a secular age, struggle to work out what we should do in the face of numerous misuses of power. In the process of working on this book, I have found entire books that address the topic of power, noting the shift toward a postcolonial interpretation of the world.[2] As we will see, this secular age can be described as a postcolonial project gripped by ongoing discussions about power, its abuses, and our inability to formulate, with consistency, how to address injustice and

---

1. Martin, "Malcolm Browne, 'Burning Monk' Photographer, Dead at 81."

2. Consider: Biggar, *Colonialism*. Or for a more theological emphasis, see Bauckham, *Bible and Mission*.

oppressive systems. There is absolutely no way of describing the present secular realities without revisiting the issue of unbalanced approaches to power.

As in the previous chapter a simple phrase summarizes our concern. "Less power and more participation" is a starting point for exploring facets of an emerging secular age. It is meant to provide handles for deeper reflection and for revisiting both our present culture and our need to move people toward a better understanding of the larger story of the Bible. In so doing, I want to provide some practical steps that will help us learn to be more sensitive to abuses of power, their links to spiritual matters, and how this is redefining our emerging secular age.

It has been my experience that if we do this with wisdom and compassion, we may be surprised to find that many in our secular age are desperately searching for a more redemptive understanding of power that Jesus, and the larger trajectory of the Bible, provides. Lastly, I hope that future attempts to address this issue will involve new models of collaboration and participation that create healthier postcolonial possibilities for exploring the gift of the Bible and hearing its teaching as essential for experiencing God's healing.

POWER AND THE ISSUE OF TRAUMA

Less power does not mean *no power*, yet many who have experienced the abuses of power need time to reflect on what a healthy view of power entails. While I want to consider these issues with the Bible in mind, we cannot ignore that misuse of power is now part of daily life. Journals like *The Harvard Business Review* document how power impacts the workplace and profits.[3] To this we can add aggressive parents who pass on unhealthy views of power at what should be playful sporting events. In addition, we all live in a digital tsunami of trauma linked to the barrage of images of global unrest, economic disparity, and countless stories of injustice linked to power struggles.

What remains particularly sad is that churches and religious leaders have not been models of hope and health in this regard. Due to abusive uses of power some in roles of spiritual authority have contributed to a cultural category we refer to as "spiritual trauma." Stories associated with the mishandling of power by religious leaders are etched into the subconscious

3. Gerhardt et al., "Harnessing the Power of Age Diversity."

of many. In Canada, I think of the terrible atrocities related to Indigenous communities,[4] a shock so unimaginable it sparked a visit from Pope Francis undertaking a "penitential pilgrimage" in the summer of 2022.[5]

How those in a secular age will piece together narratives related to abuses of power remains complex, yet we must commit to learn from these grave errors in hopes of reimagining new ways offered to us in the Bible. The late Walter Brueggemann, an exceptional scholar, calls us to a deeper place when he notes:

> While the world basically uses power to shut things down, to silence new possibility, to intimidate newness that threatens, Christians are called to notice the dangerous restlessness of God's power that shatters our complacency and overrides our despair.[6]

As part of this chapter, I will suggest that confession, compassion, and care must involve ongoing participation with diverse viewpoints for a healthy view of power to emerge. Only then will we learn that not all viewpoints are equally helpful, but all are valid enough to be heard. This, I believe, can foster healthier models of leadership that reclaim a biblical view of authority and a biblical understanding of power. Moreover, this will create a dialogue about right uses of power that avoids "authoritarian" approaches. The shifts of our secular context will require listening that rebuilds credibility if we hope to guide people into a fresh engagement with how the Bible addresses such issues.

MISUSED POWER AND MISTRUST

A young woman at our church recently shared her embarrassment to be associated with a Christian faith that has historically done so many horrible things. While listening, I wanted her to know that I too felt some of the same feelings. I agreed with her that misuses of power have led to new forms of mistrust toward leaders, teachers, and even parents who are wrestling with mistrust all the way to defiance. As we spoke, our shared honesty was a first step that I think those in a secular age are looking for. It is this awareness that helps us begin to consider what "less power" means and how confession and humility are paramount.

---

4. Mansoor, "'Deplorable' History Behind the Pope's Apology."
5. Canadian Conference of Catholic Bishops, "Pope Francis' Penitential Pilgrimage."
6. Brueggemann, *Collected Sermons*, 55.

Less Power, More Participation

As I speak with young people, I find that abuses of power are a regular part of how they process cultural issues. For many, their present responses include the need for protest. It is the law of our land that legal and respectful protest is important but more than that, it is linked to showing solidarity and participation in a vision for change. This shared human responsibility to stand in support of those hurt by abuses of power is how many in our secular age process their own pain. We can celebrate both the right and responsibility to speak up, but more will be needed. Whatever future steps we consider, addressing suspicion towards power is a key step to exploring a densely complex issue. This has huge implications for reimagining the role of the Bible and the unique message it offers in the face of injustice and unrepentant abuses of power. Moreover, an approach that takes "less power" seriously will challenge our most basic desires for control and dominance.

A common overreaction by those in power is to do everything possible to hold on to power. In so doing, those in power may misunderstand what *less power* will entail for those in a secular age. I include myself in this category since I have been blessed to sit and serve in places of positional authority, which includes a certain amount of privilege and power. Regularly, I must check myself and recall the nature of power with ongoing practices of submission, never ignoring what Galadriel, in *The Lord of the Rings*, knew oh so well: that "the hearts of men [and women] are easily corrupted."

For our present discussion, I want to propose that "less power" means more safe spaces for those who are often rendered powerless by abusive systems. Less power may involve a space to think about *shared* power for others to speak courageously when they notice possible abuses. Those in a secular age are noticing how some of our most cherished institutions, which includes the church, are at times part of the problem. Thus, less power means less trust in corporate structures that fuel greed by capitalizing on the weak and marginalized. Systems that exude power for self-preservation at the expense of people point to a particular clarion call for less power in the hands of the wrong people. But how do we develop the right kinds of people, who can be trusted to use power properly? This is the deeper task at hand. It is this question that makes our need to come back to the Bible so urgent.

I wish more people in secular age knew that the Bible addresses our human propensity to cover up and abuse power for self-interest's sake. Consider this image from a Jewish prophet: "Listen to me, you fat cows living in Samaria, you women who oppress the poor and crush the needy, and who are always calling to your husbands, 'Bring us another drink!'"[7] The intensity is shocking. The prophet chastises the people of God for their blatant apathy toward the powerless. Here "less power" involves exposing self-serving abuses of wealth.

The Bible is clear that power, when unchecked, blinds us to our complicity in supporting oppressive practices. While we return to these key themes in Part 2, I hope you already feel that a return to the Bible may in fact provide a new space to get serious about issues that are bubbling to the surface in our secular age. Moreover, it is good news that God deems it unacceptable to ignore such issues. In fact, we need those in a secular culture to know that the Bible doesn't just critique abuses but also reveals that power alone is never enough. New models are needed, and they must be linked to the voices of those who have felt powerless, and the message that God continues to empower some of the most unlikely people to play their part in addressing the shifts of this present crisis.

A flourishing future points to our human need for sustainable models of engagement around issues of power. Even when disagreeing, we will need to rebuild trust in numerous areas of society. The Bible remains essential as it points to our need for trust and truth to be linked. It will be essential for leaders to use their influence to encourage and equip others to grow so that we see a shared power dynamic that makes Jesus and his ways central, not just our agenda or perspective. The spiritually curious, as we saw in the last chapter, are exploring their questions by ignoring the old inherited power models. It is another way to speak out against misuses of power. Nevertheless, speaking out does not provide the ongoing wisdom needed to envision and create new systems that model healthy uses of power, which are linked to a biblical view of authority.

SECULAR SHIFT: INNER POWER

In his *Sources of the Self*, Charles Taylor notes how our secular age critiques power by making an internal turn. This move to "inner" power has culminated in a new dimension of power that is associated with authentic self-expression. He writes: "The modern subject is no longer defined just by the power of disengaged rational control, but by this new power of expressive self-articulation."[8] This shift is now a default way of understanding what it

---

7. Amos 4:1 (NLT).
8. Taylor, *Sources of the Self*, 390.

means to be human. Moreover, this internal view of power makes us feel strongest as we express ourselves, even if it means rejecting older models of power. Here our modern notion of the self and our claim to subjective authentic selves is affirmed as a new dimension of power.

Taylor's insights are paramount as we keep reflecting on the shifts of this secular age. Equally, I think people I interact with are showing signs of fatigue as they try to find stable and healthy models of power in the world. The harder it becomes to find a sense of stability in our surroundings, the easier we default to turning inward. This inward move soon creates new challenges, including an internal dialogue that produces unexpected pressure to define ourselves by ourselves. Surprisingly, we are left with a new sense of anxiety about our "inner self." Concepts like "the inner you," "live a centered life," "personal positivity," "your truth," and "positive energy" are just some ways we now speak about this inner dimension of power. This has come at a time when a therapeutic understanding of "the self" has converged with the billion-dollar wellness movements is now fused into the psyche of everyone born in this emerging secular context.

To some degree, we have all been shaped by this move toward inner power. Remember that the secular is not just "out there." Even those in church who read the Bible and believe in God have been impacted by the idea that we find more of God as we look into ourselves. While this is not necessarily bad, it is not fully true. The only way to address this will require better Bible teachers. It has been my experience that we may have missed an opportunity to speak about this issue in a loving and corrective way. Having missed this window, we now see signs pointing to an increased wave of popular speakers and preachers riding the personal inner power shift. This aligns with personal forms of spirituality, as discussed in chapter 1.

A pioneer of this movement was the late Robert Schuller. He was a popular TV preacher whose claim to fame was a program called *The Hour of Power*.[9] Although Schuller's program aired years ago, its relegation of power to one's inner life focused on private spirituality struck a nerve. One of the reasons it was so popular was that it was an approach to the spiritual life that was easy. Not only did the technology at the time beam the talk right into your home, but it slowly detached people from the importance of communal leadership, which involves thinking about power dynamics in relation to others. If power is just about self-help and self-identity, then we

---

9. It first aired in the 1970s and now has been given a new and modern feel by Schuller's grandson. See Hagerty, "Fast Fall for Once Mighty Megachurch."

can ignore the difficult challenges of our world where the structural misuses of power continue to do damage. It then becomes no one's problem to ask, "Who can truly be trusted with power?" Where are the future leaders being formed, tested, and trained before they are entrusted with power that would lead to empowering others?

Unfortunately, this shift to a self-centered view of power minimizes the accountable nature of communal structures that develop us into the kind of people who can be trusted with a healthy understanding of power. In the Bible this is always at the forefront of issues related to power. Community, relationships, and modes of accountability are part of how power issues are biblically addressed.[10] Less power without more participation that empowers others to grow will have dire consequences, no matter how much we address abuses of power. Moreover, it is this vision of empowering participation that unlocks the broader nature of community, accountability, and the consistent wisdom found in the Bible.

Our secular age bombards us with endless examples of those who abuse power while also avoiding accountability. We all should be bothered by this. Flashing through our minds are images of global leaders, politicians, even pastors who think they are above the law and beyond the reach of correction that fosters a healthy society. A biblical understanding of power always involves accountability and this, I believe, will be received as good news by those in a secular age. God-given responsibility is intricately linked to the biblical truth that one day we *all* give an account to God for our actions. Yet, the move to "inner power" makes it almost impossible to get serious about this blind spot in our present cultural moment. Power alone bypasses the biblical wisdom related to God-given authority grounded in accountability meant to prioritize all human flourishing. Further, when we begin to understand this, we remember that the God who gives power requires that we are witnesses of the one who accomplished God's purposes without the use of worldly power.

PATIENCE AND POWER: WHEN THE LAST ARE FIRST

Those who overreact toward the shifts we are discussing may miss the opportunities our present context provides. For many the Bible has been relegated to a prop that they associate with abuses of power even by those who promise to uphold the law. "Put your hand on the Bible and repeat

---

10. Matt 18:15–20.

after me" remains a common act used in law court proceedings that adds to our conundrum around power and our present culture. Therefore, those in our secular age are left with caricatures of the Bible, caricatures that add new hurdles we must address.

The Bible provides many ways to consider the layered complexities of power. One of the ways that Jesus awakens us to the issue is by his startling claim that "the last shall be first."[11] Instead of a deconstruction that rejects all power, Jesus offers a parable about who is responsible enough to use power well. To everyone's surprise Jesus states that those who have been mistreated and marginalized—"the last"—will one day be given a place of authority as the "first." They, in some ways, become those who can be trusted with *his* authority and, while they may *seem* powerless now, their participation in God's kingdom is inevitable.

Put another way, Jesus empowers those who have seen things from lowly places, painful spaces, places where "worldly" power has done its worst. Because of what Jesus does, the "lowly" will be given a voice of authority. Now, "the first" are not kicked out, but they are instructed to remember that one day they will be last. This is a gracious act of participation that points to correction and maturity. Those who are first still have lots to learn and that involves being led by those who once were last. Because the "lowly" are often most familiar with abuses of power, they will be offered a special place of spiritual authority one day. Why? I propose it is because they can be trusted in a way that aligns us with God's coming kingdom. This shocking reversal may in fact be a key to holding together the tensions emerging in our new secular contexts and our struggles with power.

"Less power" involves a reversal that includes a shared vision of power. The parable of Jesus associated with "the last being first" had to do with power in the context of work. Those who heard him say "one day the last will be first" would have been shocked.[12] What will "the last" do when they are first? How will they act? Will they use their power for revenge, to get even? Those in a secular age are unaware of how meaningful the parables of Jesus were in bypassing the regular rebuttals of the religious establishment of Jesus' day. More importantly, helping people return to the Bible will reveal that Jesus himself cares about the complex challenges of our secular age and its disordered approach to power. Jesus' parables were, and still are,

---

11. Matt 20:16.
12. Matt 20:16.

foundational for us to see ourselves in the larger unfolding story of God's redemptive plan, which includes accountability and participation.

Imagine workers in a vineyard. Think of the sweat, sore backs, and the daily struggle to survive. Jesus describes an owner of the vineyard who uses his power to be generous even when it doesn't seem fair. At the end of the day, he pays all the workers as he sees fit. One worker tells the owner of the vineyard that this lavished and gracious generosity is unfair. How could all the workers be paid the *same* wages for the day when some worked less and some worked more? The conflict over how the owner uses his power ensues. The owner states:

> "I am not being unfair to you, friend. Didn't you agree to work for a denarius? Take your pay and go. I want to give the one who was hired last the same as I gave you. Don't I have the right to do what I want with my own money? Or are you envious because I am generous?" [Jesus said,] So the last will be first, and the first will be last.[13]

This is a parable oozing with grace. Here is the gift of generous provision bestowed on each of us no matter when we show up and how much we have to offer. It corrects a power dynamic that leads one to believe that our position means we deserve more than another. Notably, Jesus is not providing a commentary on the importance of hard work, but he is getting at a kind of power associated with God's grace. This vision of the kingdom that Jesus inaugurates reverses our categories of power and position for something more beautiful that can only be captured by understanding that even the last will one day be made to feel dignity and worth. Abuses of power are exposed as foolish and temporary. This redefinition of a good use of power and influence is what a secular age needs more than ever. It is one that reminds us that even the powerless are not forgotten when the Bible is embraced as the living truth.

Around the world, Christians continue to model this courageous kingdom vision of power in complex spaces as they live and work in abusive settings. I have been blessed to see "the last and lowly" firsthand as I visited sisters and brothers in poverty-stricken regions of the world. It is here that I started to see even the our secular approaches, often seen as First World, were no match for the joy and hope of those we often associate with being last. It is a reminder of what God can do in the face of abuses of power. Many live in places where being last means being voiceless, abused,

---

13. Matt 20:13–16.

marginalized, and even martyred. Some become heroes by paying the cost for calling out injustice. Former Archbishop of El Salvador and revered saint and martyr Oscar Romero reminded us that "there are many things that can only be seen through the eyes that have cried." He was assassinated for calling out injustice and remains a powerful prophetic voice for us to recognize that "last" may see more clearly than we thought.

DID POWER PRODUCE THE BIBLE?

While a secular age filled with abuses of power needs to learn from Jesus' healing ways, we may have to take a step back to help those who struggle because of distorted views related to how we actually got the Bible. I do not think we can assume this will just go away. Captured by the phrase "history is written by the winners," those in a secular culture wonder about the Bible and whether those in power manipulated the process that gave us our Bible. If history is truly written *only* by the winners, then some will continue to conclude that the Bible has unhealthy ties to power-hungry leaders who silenced those they did not like and then used their abusive ways to put the Bible they wanted together.

This is the underlying plot of the 2006 blockbuster movie *The Da Vinci Code* and the many online offshoot conspiracy theories that use a similar argument. The movie links power and religious leaders. One scene vividly depicts a secret meeting with a character called the "teacher." The tension builds to a secret revelation about how church leaders bent on keeping their power manipulate matters related to the Bible. Keep in mind that this is Hollywood. The "teacher" character, acting like a historian, played by Sir Leigh Teabing, states: "The Good Book did not arrive by facsimile from heaven. The Bible, as we know it, was finally presided over by one man: the Pagan emperor Constantine."

While real historians know this never happened, it now has become a refrain for many who are unsure about the Bible. Further, many are convinced the church and the Bible are linked to strange and secretive power games. Almost twenty years since this movie came out, I still hear similar stories linking power of an emperor with strange tales about the Bible. While I jokingly respond that any book from such a pagan emperor should not be described as "good," I still find this cultural myth deeply embedded in our secular subconscious.

In fact the Emperor Constantine had nothing to do with the books that make up our Bible. While he remains controversial for repositioning Christianity for unimaginable influence, this should not negate three hundred years of Christian leaderships before Constantine ever came to power. Moreover, we know that the earliest followers of Jesus who were hearing, copying, and sharing the words of the Bible were *participants* in communal worship as they faced injustice and oppression in the ancient world. In fact, Christians had letters circulating in their midst that we now have in our Bible. This took place centuries before the Emperor Constantine's influence and thus should cause us to pause and reconsider when we hear talk about the Bible in line with the phrase "history is written by the winners." Lastly, some of the leaders linked to the Bible were martyrs and models of humility as sacrificial partners in the gospel. While there is *some* truth to the phrase that winners and power are enmeshed in some historical records, it does not capture what we know about the earliest texts of the Bible.

Simplistic retellings of early Christianity are often built on half-truths and need to be corrected. This is one part of how we help those in a secular age trust that the Bible as we rightfully address and acknowledge abuses of power. Thankfully new research is putting a spotlight on our need to correct Hollywoodized versions of the Bible and the early church.[14] For a secular culture predisposed to see power struggles at every turn, it is important to acknowledge wrongful uses of power in the name of religion, while addressing strange assumptions and fictitious stories about power when dealing with the nature of the Bible.

The first step to correct distortions related to the Bible is to get honest. It is true that the "Good Book" did not just fall from the sky. The letters in the New Testament were compiled over many years, and originally used in worship settings for both encouragement and instruction in local churches. For that reason, it took time to bring them all together in a way that would be trustworthy for all Christians. Subsequently, the books which were recognized as trustworthy revealed the true things about Jesus that many leaders already knew, having heard them orally. An underlying truth about Jesus had to do with a reversal of power, about a God who did not use brute power to accomplish his purposes. Instead, he sent his only begotten

---

14. Vince Bantu has written insightfully about what we can learn from other cultures. See his *Multitude of All Peoples*. See also Fairbairn, *Global Church*.

Less Power, More Participation

Son as a servant, who would redefine both authority and our most distorted views of power."[15]

If power was used to put the Bible together, misguided narratives argue, picking and choosing which books to put in the Bible would have been much easier than what we know happened. As a substitute for the prayer, patience, and discernment that the church required to *recognize* which books could be trusted, forceful manipulation would have made things much easier. In fact, the actual, slow process of canonization would have been quick. Thankfully, what actually took place was a gradual attentiveness to key makers, authors, and communities mixed with discernment and participation by local communities. One of those markers involved the sharing of letters. As Paul states: "After you have read this letter, pass it on to the church at Laodicea so they can read it, too. And you should read the letter I wrote to them."[16]

Secondly, the ancient writings which made it into our Bible depict a God who is powerful and loving, caring and merciful at the same time. For instance, the psalmist prayed: "One thing God has spoken, two things I have heard: 'Power belongs to you, God, and with you, Lord, is unfailing love.'"[17] Those in a secular age may not see this at first glance. This is understandable if all they hear is a strange media-saturated view of our Bible. Nevertheless, the God we meet in the Bible uses his power to empower us to be involved in his purposes even in the process of providing us with a Bible. It is good news that it pleases him to have us, his human creation, with all of our flaws and shortcomings, participate in his restoring plan.

Let me be honest, if I had angels at my disposal, I would never have included messy, mistake-prone humans to do anything. Nonetheless, God did not use power-hungry rulers to force-feed us the Bible. This is one of the unique features of the Bible. It calls us to remember how even the most powerful God is sensitive to the frailty of humans and yet longs to see them find their place in his redemptive ways. As we all know, aggressive uses of power would have been easier and quicker, yet they would have been inconsistent with the nature of the God that Jesus came to reveal to us.

The Bible, when read properly, reveals a God who does not always use his power to unilaterally accomplish things. Instead, he draws near to help us know we too can experience his power in a way that is foreign to our

---

15. Phil 2.
16. Col 4:16.
17. Ps 62:11–12.

secular contexts. Here we are all invited to see restoration, responsibility, and the possibilities of using power in redemptive ways. Hence, participation and power are brought together in a way that fosters healing. Also, this shared vision of power moves us closer to the biblical idea of godly authority. Whatever new myths about the Bible and abuses of power await, may we be wise to recognize that many of those who were selected to write, pass on, carry, read, and copy the documents that came together as the Bible, died as martyrs at the hands of ruthless power-hungry rulers. They knew firsthand the need for less power and more participation.

THE MESSINESS OF PARTICIPATION

Years ago, a mentor offered his wisdom to help me in one of my first roles as a lead pastor. He knew how to give advice when a decision might have unforeseen consequences. He never told me what to do, yet he had a gift for helping me to learn how to think about the outcomes of my choices. This is one of my early memories of how to handle authority and influence as a spiritual leader. By now you should know that I write not as a professional who always knows what to do, but from an awareness that I still have many lessons to learn.

On one occasion, I was thinking of how to lead in a way that involved more of our teenagers in our Sunday morning worship gathering. I wanted to model how power and influence in the local church could be used to make room for the next generation. My idea involved creating room for others who felt that their perspective and participation did not matter. My "genius" idea was to invite the youth of the church to serve as a part of an upcoming communion celebration.

Aware of the different ways that Christians approach this sacred meal, I made time to discuss the issue with my mentor. He could tell that I wanted the worship experience to be both reverent and hopeful about the future. As we discussed the research about young people and their disillusionment with church, he listened and helped me think about what a healthy use of power and authority might entail.[18] Moreover, from personal experience, I remember that when I participated in the life of the church, I was more likely to see how important pastoral leadership was for the health of the larger church community.

18. Earls, "Most Teenagers Drop Out of Church."

Less Power, More Participation

My mentor was a great sounding board for whether I was going too far or too fast. In the end, he said, "You should try it and trust that the people will see your heart for God and his work." Well, he was wrong. What I did not anticipate was the unpredictable aspects of participation. Two of our youth who agreed to serve communion that day wore baseball caps. While I got to one of them in time and he removed his casual headwear, the other stood by the communion table helping with the bread with his cap on. I knew this would come back to bite me. Although it was a miss on my part, I also knew that for young people and their families influenced by our secular age, participating in worship, even if messy, was paramount. While some interpreted what I did as irreverence, I understood and apologized but didn't stop looking for other ways to increase people's participation.

My short story about participation focuses on my shortcomings in church leadership, but I still think we will need new and creative ways to create shared participatory experiences. This idea is firmly in the Bible and it pleases God when his people, in all their diversity, act as a growing and flourishing body, to reveal that worldly uses of power have lost their grip on us because of what Jesus is doing in us. My commitment to participation has only increased as I think about the nature of leadership and power in the secular context where I serve now.

POWER AND THE NATURE OF LANGUAGE

In Quebec, debates about power are often linked to questions about language. One estimate is that almost 70 percent of vulgar profanities in French are based on church words. For example, "*tabarnak*" is a very vulgar word when used in Quebec and stems from the word for tabernacle in the Bible.[19] In addition, we live in constant tensions about French vs. English and their links to immigration, economics, and education. It might sound surprising, but this has helped me read the Bible with a particular awareness of the language challenges the earliest Christians probably had to deal with.

Remember, in the biblical context, the Greek, Hebrew, and Latin cultures came with their own language, customs, and modes of understanding. This surely involved power struggles, likely similar to the ones we face in a secular age that links power to what linguistic philosophers describe as a

---

19. Venne, "Swearing is a Sacred Affair in Quebec."

postmodern attention to language. This includes resistance toward those in power who have made themselves the gatekeepers of language.[20]

In a remarkable book called *Abuse of Language—Abuse of Power*, Josef Pieper revisits this challenge around language and power during the time of Plato and his struggles with the Sophists. The Sophists were teachers who played loose with words, bending them and claiming that words did not really point to reality, suggesting that we cannot really know what is true about the world. Plato's critique to this group of teachers stated: "You can give fine speeches, but you simply cannot join in a conversation; you are incapable of dialogue!"[21] The insight is clear. Power games and word games make it hard for us to discuss and dialogue in ways that move us toward solutions. The same is unfolding today in our tensions about less power, more power, no power, whose power.

Plato's response has gripped me as one of the unintended consequences of the church in a secular age. Plato put his finger on what we feel. Dialogue, at least meaningful dialogue, requires that we agree on a healthy and honest use of language. We will squeeze ourselves out of being able to have new and constructive conversations that impact hearing and understanding the Bible properly if we do not consider how language and abuses of power cloud our judgment. Power games get in the way of how shared language is meant to guide our participation for finding solutions through the painful shifts of our emerging secular age.

Astutely, Pieper observes that if cultures do not correct abuses of language, so that words point *truthfully* to the world around us, only raw power is left.[22] This is at stake in our growing secular culture and our longing for less power, squashing our ability to participate in meaningful dialogue. Correcting unhealthy uses of power must include increasingly healthy uses of power that cultivate trust and foster diverse ideas around participation. This must be done as words and their meaning are restored to what is true and real about our present context. The influx of digital distortion will only increase our need for reliable spaces for trust and truth that call out abuses of power. Journalist Petra P. Sebek touches on new spiritualties related to the web and the interactive nature of social media. What she reveals is new terms, stretching language, which include "cyber-spirituality" and "digital

---

20. Moati, *Derrida/Searle*.
21. Pieper, *Abuse of Language, Abuse of Power*.
22. This was Friedrich Nietzsche's argument.

religion," pointing to our human longing to participate with what may be beyond the here and now.[23]

The focus on the Bible and the story it tells about us reveals how those empowered by the Holy Spirit lived at a time when they too had to rearticulate and translate the stories of the Bible in shifting times. They had to reimagine language in the face of power. This included how they would speak, think, share, and talk about Jesus while providing a vision of a transformed culture. Our emerging secular context will require that we do likewise.

Throughout history every generation, with all its benefits and weaknesses, has had to revisit the gospel and reflect on fresh ways to engage with the Bible. The most formative biblical story around language is linked to the day of Pentecost. It was a day we forever equate with a renewed vision of participation, when diverse language issues are celebrated as good, and this in a world that used power to limit the voices of others. May we rest assured that whatever challenges await us, those who have come before us navigated similar struggles all in the name of God's unimaginable blessing and power.

THE FUTURE: AUTHORITY AND INFLUENCE THAT REDEFINES POWER

For those serious about engaging in secular spaces, we must model with consistency that sin is not just out there in the world but also part of why Christians mishandle power. Thus, less power and more participation is shaped by a biblical truth of our need to remain rooted in a sacrificial way of life with others in mind. Those in a secular society do not understand that the Christian faith, at its inception, flourished without the benefits of oppressive levers of power. To this day, many still wonder how Christianity took shape and subsequently how the Bible played a pivotal role in the growth of the faith. It never gets old to remember an adage from a leading early church scholar who remarked: "We name our dogs Nero and our sons Paul."[24]

It has never been more urgent to reclaim a kind of influence, including authority, that does not grasp for power. Only this creates new spaces for safe and joyful participation. We cannot ignore that anything less, in this present secular context, will be experienced as abusive uses of power.

23. Scbek, *Spirituality in the Selfie Culture*.
24. Bruce, *Paul*, 5.

Rebuilding trust with those in our communities who have formed numerous assumptions about the Bible due to its negative uses will require a new paradigm. It is my hope that we can reimagine the kind of influence informed by humility that reveals that worldly power is not a prerequisite to being the people of God who participate in work that honors Jesus. Furthermore, it has been my experience that those who do not long for power are most likely the best candidates to be entrusted to wield it wisely.

Former prime minister of Kenya Jomo Kenyatta allegedly remarked: "When the missionaries came to Africa, they had the Bible, and we had the land. They said: 'let us close our eyes and pray.' When we opened them, we had the Bible, and they had the land." For those in secular culture, it is undeniable that power, religion, and the Bible make for a perfect cocktail of suspicion. Although we may come to the Bible with the trust that it is the *authoritative* word of God, those in secular age will wonder what that will mean when power is involved. We cannot underestimate how misuse of the Bible skews what healthy views of authority entail.

In the Letter to the Colossians, we are guided to reconsider strange views of power in light of the spiritual authority modeled by Jesus. Paul writes:

> For in Christ all the fullness of the Deity lives in bodily form, and in Christ you have been brought to fullness. He is the head over every power and authority . . . having been buried with him in baptism, in which you were also raised with him through your faith in the working of God, who raised him from the dead.[25]

We often glance over the kind of influence God is offering. It is one that holds together power and authority when dealing with the invisible world of cosmic spiritual conflict. To our surprise we are told that invisible powers are not to be combatted only in the spiritual realm. Instead, "the powers" are dealt with as we participate with God in our present lived reality. Put simply, a correct view of power requires presence. Jesus' presence among humanity was how the spiritual matters were dealt with. By presence, we are invited to recall our own baptism and the need for intimate proximity to relationships. Again, the biblical passage draws us deeper into human presence by inviting us to remember the mystery of our own baptism, a body washed and raised, fully present, and fully alive again.

---

25. Col 2:9–11.

Less Power, More Participation

Participation, in this rich biblical sense, rejects the disembodied narrative of what it means to be human. Therefore, we are wise to remember that God's ways involve celebrating the gift of our humanity. For Christians, the apex of this truth is rooted in the doctrine of the incarnation. In Jesus, incarnate, all forms of abusive power are disarmed and rendered powerless. This is a doctrinal truth the sets us on a path toward dismantling the powers of an abusive world. When the next generation struggling amid the shifts of a secular age starts to understand this, it will begin to loosen the grip that often leads to despair. A God who took on flesh remains our model for contesting corruption of power in all its disordered ways. In the same chapter, Paul continues: "And having disarmed the powers and authorities, he made a public spectacle of them, triumphing over them by the cross."[26] May we never forget that Jesus disarms the powers by revealing their uselessness against his selfless ways.

My prayer is that the complexities explored in this chapter will remind us that we need to inspire a new movement that returns to the Bible as we acknowledge the real power struggles we face. Our "solutions" will never arise from wrong assumptions about our secular age. Moreover, this will fuel wrong assumptions about the Bible and the issues of power that require our attention. We will not be able to just preach our way out of this present reality rooted in the power of God's living truth found in the Bible. What will be required is fruitful patterns of participation that involve less abusive and misaligned uses of power. To this we must add the wisdom of Lesslie Newbigin, who asserts, "It will not do to say simply, 'the Bible tells me so' if you cannot give reasons for the Bible rather than the Qur'an, Gita or *Das Capital*."[27] The reasons we give will come from the great stories found in the Bible that reveal a God who came down to restore our world by participating in it. Any other approach, set on triumphal proclamations, will continually be interpreted as longing for more power.

---

26. Col 2:15.
27. Newbigin, *Foolishness to the Greeks*, 11.

CHAPTER 3

Less Telling, More Teaching

"If the gospel is proclaimed in a language that our culture cannot understand . . . then the church has failed in its mission."—Alister McGrath

BURNING BIBLES AND BURNING QUESTIONS

WHEN I WAS A teenager conflicts about religion were common in our home. On one occasion, my uncle became increasingly frustrated with our family's connection with a new church, a Protestant church. Up to that point our family had only been part of a Roman Catholic church. While my early experiences within the Roman Catholic Church were positive, the complex heritage of Quebec put Roman Catholics and Protestants always at odds with each other. These debates often had unspoken tensions related to our identity as a family, our European roots, and many confusing beliefs about the Bible.

One evening remains symbolic of the kind of fighting that "religious" anger and an underdeveloped understanding of the Bible can produce. In such moments, we were often *told* what to believe. This provided little room to consider the larger history of Christianity and the changes we were experiencing by attending a new church. As is still true today, my family, and in this case my uncle, was not equipped to make sense of different interpretations, let alone the cultural shifts we have been exploring in this book. We were just *told* who was right, who was wrong, and who to avoid along the way.

As part of this particular tense conversation my uncle abruptly yelled: "Get me the Bibles!" There could have been about three, maybe four, that someone quickly found in the house. His anger and frustration was tied to the fact that some in our family had started attending a Protestant church which he connected to our new interest in reading the Bible. This was seen as disloyal. As a statement of control meant to tell us what to do, he threw the Bibles into the fireplace. After a gasp, the room went silent. There was a slow-mo, surreal feel about it all as the crackly sound of burning Bibles filled the room. I did not dare say a word, but man, did I have questions. Didn't Catholics read and care about the Bible? Were there curses associated with burning religious books? How could burning Bibles be a sign of one's commitment to the Catholic faith? Was God going to punish our family because of my uncle's actions?

That intense evening remains etched in my mind as an example of how change reveals deep-seated assumptions about beliefs. Moreover, it was indicative of a culture of *telling* people what to do and what to believe. While this is a pattern used with young children who cannot understand challenging ideas, it will not be sustainable if we—as adults—hope to address the shifts of a secular age. One painful outcome of these struggles was that many in my extended family slowly disassociated from the Christian faith and soon became disinterested in the Bible.

You may have your own stories of confusion and frustration around religion. The joke that we should not address politics and religion together is revealing of the kinds of people we have become. Further, it speaks to the state of a secular world that has less and less space for real and deep learning, yet will need it to make sense of the life we were meant to live. As our views and beliefs are contested, long-held assumptions about faith, God, religion, church, and the Bible will lead to unexpected conflict. In this chapter, I want to suggest that we reject the attitudes and fears that cultivate a "tell" approach to faith. Those shaped by a secular age have developed a robust resistance against those who tell people what to believe. Accordingly, I want to unpack ways we should do less telling and more teaching.

The more one interacts within emerging secular spaces, the more aware one becomes of an internal paradox around contested worldviews. As we have seen, this is informed by an attitude of confrontation and infighting. One goal of this book has been to reconsider the shifts of a secular age and how they might lead to new spaces of learning. In his important book on competing worldviews, David T. Koyzis remarks:

> Since virtually the beginning of the Christian era, believers have sought to think through and articulate an approach to the larger

culture that is faithful to the imperatives of the gospel yet recognizes that by God's grace there is much to be learned from that culture.[1]

Koyzis's thoughts are helpful since a secular age is part of our larger culture and we can and should learn to see even the challenges it poses as a call toward a deeper appreciation of God's grace that draws us back to the Bible. Minimizing the posture of learning that is required will lead to constant feelings of doubt. Moreover, it blinds us to the fact that our culture is always changing, and we are wise to develop an approach that can adapt and change as we trust God's leading. This is an essential biblical truth.

Accordingly, I want to explore some guiding principles for why *less telling and more teaching* provides a framework for how to address our secular age's shifts in learning. We are living at a time when more and more people equate Christians with being judgemental and close-minded. While I know this is not fair, it does ring true for those in our present culture who often experience silly and foolish examples of what it means to be a Christian. The algorithms rarely bring to the surface thoughtful, kind, and wise teachers. In addition, we all know of examples of forceful "preacher" types who just tell people what to do and what to believe. While "telling" may be helpful in some cases, those in a secular age often interpret it as close-minded religious arrogance. As we reflect on what less telling means, I propose that this shift will guide us to see when those in a secular age are open and curious to the kind of teaching that is shaped by authentic, honest, and mutual learning. Less telling is just one way we can cultivate thoughtful teaching approaches that allow us to reconsider important ideas about the Bible.

Few in our secular age know that the Bible reveals Jesus as a great teacher. While for many he was just a teacher, even fewer would know that one of Jesus' last commands to his followers was that they would go and feed/teach those learning how to follow in his ways.[2] In my experience, conversations that foster *more* teaching must include hearing the kind of questions that people have. It can be easy to teach what we know without listening to the actual questions people have. The three handles I have provided in Part 1 of this book have tried to frame a space for thinking that leads to the new questions bubbling up from those in a secular culture.

---

1. Koyzis, *Political Visions*, 182.
2. John 21:17.

Less Telling, More Teaching

Many people I speak with have so many great questions about Jesus, spirituality, faith in God, and the Bible. As I listen, I too am learning that my assumptions about what truly is secular may also need to adapt and change. This has convinced me that we will need new narratives of why people do not believe rather than old caricatures. In this sense, "more teaching" is about mutual learning. As I have listened to those visiting church for the first time, or doubting the Bible, it has forced me to reframe how I speak about what I believe. For some, less telling and more teaching may seem frustrating. It involves somewhat of an improvisational approach to teaching rather than a firm lecture-type of telling. However, this shift will reveal new opportunities that can speak to the painful isolation, fragmentation, and disruptions at the heart of a secular age.

As we explore these themes, I want to assure you that those in a secular age do realize that they have lots to learn. The bigger challenge will be whether we are forming the kinds of teachers, parents, pastors that are trustworthy. Further, I want to show how more teaching helps us reclaim a proper understanding of the Bible. To do so, I will revisit the important idea of *sola scriptura* and what that might mean for less telling and more teaching. This matters if we hope to teach from the Bible in a way that the living words are heard as living truth from a living God. Unless we can cultivate approaches the involve less telling and more teaching, we remain ill-equipped to face those formed by a secular age.

LESS TELLING AND MORE LISTENING *FIRST*

After completing my PhD, I foolishly believed I had earned the right to "tell" people what I knew. I had forgotten that my research was not enough to earn the right to tell people things. My studies in historical theology did not magically wash away the cultural attitudes steeped in relational fragmentation, religious tribalism, and distrust that runs deep in a secular age. Even more, I was not aware that telling people about God or even the Bible when they were not ready or interested only strengthened their resistance. Hence, becoming aware of this has been a constant lesson.

It might come as a shock, but both in and out of church, people are likely to ignore, and sometimes even mock, those who tell them what to believe or what to do. We have a natural reflex that causes us to ignore those we feel are telling us what to do. Moreover, some believe that since they can consult a Bible, and thus can find the info they need when they are ready, why would anyone have to tell them what to do? These ideas shape us into people who reject modes of instruction as arrogant. Also, the internet has rewired us to think we can learn when and from whom we like. As we become more aware of our *telling* tendencies, we will also notice that just telling people about God or the Bible causes them not to listen well. Here, the biblical wisdom to be "slow to speak and quick to listen" should be our guide.[3]

The approach to listening I am suggestng implies that we listen to learn, understand, and become aware of what kind of teaching is needed. We listen to hear what kind of questions are truly being asked. Our secular age is revealing things that we might not want to hear but we should. In fact, if we are truly listening, we may hear more clearly what the researchers of *Leaving Christianity* highlight. That is: "The research shows that many youth and young adults haven't even been exposed to Christianity . . . The result is a religious landscape that we have never seen before."[4] Consider that in a short period of time, we have seen a new generation experience a shift that is even more startling than the sheer rejection of Christian beliefs. In fact, as I often remark, many in a secular age do not even care to attack our belief. They distrust religion and indifference and ignorance have replaced their active anger toward faith issues.

Just to clarify, less telling does not mean we never speak up with boldness. Nonetheless, we will all have to pause long enough to listen and know when our boldness will be misunderstood as boasting. This middle space involves discerning when forceful truth-telling is needed and when disciplined silence is also God-honoring. Because a secular age creates an instinctual resistance to telling models, we are wise to pursue the kind of patience often exhibited by Jesus himself.[5] As noted earlier, when power struggles are assumed, telling is interpreted as dominance. This is something that even preachers and teachers may miss. My suggestion is that we acknowledge that in a secular age telling approaches, especially in the context of faith and the Bible, are rejected as insensitive. You might love your opinions, as I do mine, but to tell them, post them, and share them as

---

3. Jas 1:19.

4. Clarke and Macdonald, *Leaving Christianity*, 26.

5. I think of how the greatest teacher patiently spent three years with the same guys to help them rethink how they had heard and understood the story of Israel. "How long must I put up with you?" (Matt 17:17).

Less Telling, More Teaching

the dominant or only way to engage with others sabotages the crucial and creative spaces needed to teach.

Recently, a first-time guest at our church shared about something that made it difficult for them to come back to church. As I've explained, I want to model listening to what is being said. They had first watched our gatherings online and slowly found the courage to come and visit in person. Their previous experience with church involved a preacher telling him that God would punish their family if they did not start to give more money. My heart sank as I knew that was not how the Bible addressed the important matter of money. Stories like this have caused me to also learn that whenever people experience peaching as forceful telling they soon struggle to hear and understand the good and helpful teaching of the Bible, due to an inner trauma brought about by telling tactics.

In this sense, less telling means more empathy with people who are trying to heal from the abusive uses of the Bible that distorted the good things the Bible teaches us. In my own leadership journey this meant that less telling would involve getting lower and closer rather than louder. Louder preaching, when aggressive, must be replaced with getting closer to the questions, the concerns, the pains, and the doubts. Here telling is substituted for a form of listening that is rooted in patience, that creates room for discerning when more teaching is required. As Jesus warned, even a good seed can fail to take root if other circumstances have clouded one's mind.[6]

Empathy involves patience. This is not only for those who are struggling "out there" in the world. It is also a patient awareness for listening to what is being said at our kitchen tables with a son or granddaughter. I often advise parents on how natural and important healthy spiritual maturity includes new questions that point to deeper doubts. This might be sparked by a class in university, coffee with a friend, or a documentary on Netflix. Less telling fosters room for the next generation, fully engaging with secular realities, to question what they were once told as they develop in their faith. When we are not equipped for this kind of listening, just telling becomes a default of our own fears. When this happens, telling kids what to believe stirs up a defensiveness that those in a secular age associate with weakness. If the gospel is true, they remark, why are we so nervous when our questions put it to the test? It has been my experience that instead of cultivating space for deeper teaching moments, many often rush to tell. This is a huge

---

6. Luke 8:11–15.

blind spot if we hope to pass on the faith to those shaped by the many assumptions of a shifting secular culture.

All of this comes on the heels of a slow collapse of traditional modes of learning. By "traditional," I do not mean bad, but instead approaches to learning that are predominantly top-down. While approaches that use mostly telling will not vanish, they promote obedience out of fear, rather than obedience out of joy and transformation. If we are truly listening, we will not miss the major shifts in learning brought about by a digital revolution. This is essential as we reflect on defining what more teaching will entail.

Almost thirty years ago, Neil Postman wrote *Amusing Ourselves to Death*. It is still a watershed work pointing to shifts related to learning, listening, and teaching. His warning was that learning should not be confused with entertainment. In fact, he coined a new term, *edutainment*, to address issues he noticed due to the invention of TV. Imagine if he could see things now. In a secular context, shifts we must grapple with are more like a tsunami of new consequences that will undoubtedly impact the way people read, understand, and apply the Bible. At its core, we cannot miss that with all great shifts in society we must come back to *how* we learn just as much as *what* we should learn. In this sense, the shifts of our secular age may provide helpful points of rediscovery if we are truly listening.

THE NATURE OF MORE TEACHING?

A recent report from Japan noted a government initiative using robots in 500 classrooms to help teach English.[7] Imagine what robotics, AI, and other new models of teaching will mean if we do not reconsider less telling and more teaching at a root level. Not only will we miss a teaching revolution taking shape right before our eyes, but we will forget that throughout history, leaders who loved the Bible were most keen to adopt pioneering ways that would lead to better teaching that engaged a changing culture. This is true from manuscript technology like the codex in the first century to newer technologies like the printing press in the fifteenth century. Furthermore, the invention of the eyeglasses and the innovation we call Sunday school are just a few examples that reveal the church's ability to adapt to the need of new forms of teaching. Whenever we get serious about the Bible,

---

7. *The Straits Times*, "Japan Classrooms to Use AI Robots."

Less Telling, More Teaching

the church has always modeled less telling, more listening and adapting in teaching approaches. Our secular age will be no different.

An approach that involves more teaching involves a consistent recommitment to embodied teaching. Naturally, if you read the Bible, you know that Jesus, who is described in the Bible as God with us, provides the greatest example of being an embodied teacher.[8] He was fully enfleshed, fully present, fully human, and yet fully divine. He taught in a way that people of his day could understand. A common Hebrew title for him was *rabboni*, meaning teacher. In hearing him many mentioned that they had never had a spiritual teacher who embodied the fullness of God for them the way Jesus did.

Luke writes about one of Jesus' earliest sermons:

> He stood up to read, and the scroll of the prophet Isaiah was handed to him. Unrolling it, he found the place where it is written: "The Spirit of the Lord is on me, because he has anointed me to proclaim good news to the poor. He has sent me to proclaim freedom for the prisoners and recovery of sight for the blind, to set the oppressed free, to proclaim the year of the Lord's favor." Then he rolled up the scroll, gave it back to the attendant and sat down. The eyes of everyone in the synagogue were fastened on him. He began by saying to them, "Today this scripture is fulfilled in your hearing."[9]

Jesus didn't just teach the truth; he was the truth fully embodied. Although we can never equate ourselves with Jesus, we are called to imitate him even as we admit our deficiencies. In Christianity, we must come back to the kind of teaching that affirms that the truth of our faith is embodied in a person before it is recorded in a book.

For too long, we have read and used the Bible and missed the deep and essential reality of embodiment for understanding the truth. This happens because telling approaches are our dominant default. When we revert to modes of telling we may in fact dehumanize the way God created us to learn. While we might be able to tell or email someone certain types of information, the kind of teaching that the Bible offers almost always requires embodiment as a visible expression of the truth. In a secular age, there is no bypassing how urgent and important this needs to be reclaimed. Put

---

8. I am in no way trying to imply that he was just a teacher.
9. Luke 4:16–21.

another way, no one is truly formed as a disciple of Jesus by just resorting to digital tools that foster a telling approach to learning.

In addition to embodied teaching, it has never been more important to realize that a secular age is one that continues to redefine paradigms of education. We are becoming increasingly aware that a classroom doesn't require a teacher to walk the talk. In recent years, AI and other tools have revolutionized the way we learn. Whether these are all good is still left to be seen, but it is more clear than ever that the spiritual formation that the Bible invites us into is much more unique.

The late Eugene Peterson put his finger on this distinctiveness of teaching about the Bible by using the image that the Bible is a book we eat. He notes, "There is a certain kind of writing that invites this kind of reading . . . as we taste and savor, anticipate and take in the sweet and spicy, mouthwatering, and soul-energizing morsel words . . ."[10] The image of eating is helpful as we come to grips with the fact that millennials, roughly those born between 1981 and 1996, are the most educated demographic in North American history. What this means is that they have been raised with consistent shifts in learning and have embraced new models of teaching for most of their lives. This cannot be ignored when we address the uniqueness of the Bible and how it addresses modern issues that concern us.

TEACHER AND ENTRUSTED VOICES

The largest and most educated generation in our history will also come with expectations about knowledge, how it is applied, and who can be trusted to teach. You may have heard that secular culture is built on a hermeneutic of suspicion. This is true partly because we have seen a slow disappearance of teachers who embody integrity and character. Further, this aggravates our suspicion towards information, knowledge, news, etc. In my experience, this does not mean that those in a secular age do not want to learn, but it will require more time to ease their concerns around who they will trust to teach them.

Telling is easy, teaching is hard. This vision of more teaching will require our constant attention if we hope to engage with the shifts of a secular age and return to important discussions about the role of the Bible. We will need embodied and trustworthy people in diverse spheres of learning—from parents, to trusted aunts or uncles, to teachers and coaches. We

---

10. Peterson, *Eat This Book*, 2.

Less Telling, More Teaching

will have to rework the whole apparatus. Christians have a rich legacy of dealing with this kind of change. In the early church several leaders gained trust because of how their lives modeled truthfulness in alignment with the teaching of Jesus in a time of rapid change. Learning from them may provide important insight about how trusted voices became paramount for explaining difficult doctrines.

Scholars often refer to these early leaders as the apostolic fathers and mothers. They hold a special place in our history for being the first to work on clarifying essential doctrines of the faith and realizing that teaching had to adapt to the shifting realities of language, rulers, and critiques Christians were facing. To this day, some of these teachers hold a trusted place for their biblical commentary and ongoing apologetic astuteness during the first few centuries of the Christian faith. It is my sense that engaging with a secular age will require we revisit not only our love for the Bible and its special place, but how our earliest Bible teachers were doing what we must do again for our time.

Just as is the case today, some of the changes the early leaders faced were deeply concerning.[11] Much was at stake as they attempted to teach the truth of Jesus rather than reverting to just telling people about Jesus. We know that some of those entrusted to teach were students of rhetoric, philosophy, law, and theology who believed that God had left tools from diverse fields of learning worth using if they could help explain the Bible in a fresh ways. Moreover, they reveal an unfathomable reverence for the Scriptures and for the shifting culture of their day. They listened to both in a way that allowed them to dialogue, engage, and teach rather than just tell. They knew that telling would not be enough to faithfully present the Bible to those who did not yet understand Jesus and his ways.

Stanley Hauerwas offers some wise words on this subject. He pinpoints what is essential about those whose lives provide a kind of teaching:

> Christians are often tempted . . . to say more than we know . . . As a result we end up saying more than we know because what we believe—or better, what we do—cannot be explained but only shown. The word we have been given for such a showing is "witness."[12]

---

11. Tertullian's concern that Athens (the world of cultural learning) and Jerusalem (the world of biblical wisdom) were at odds is likely meant as a frustration. However, Tertullian's concerns did not keep him from addressing cultural issues of his day. Tertullian was heard but not fully followed as wise counsel on this point.

12. Hauerwas, *Cross-Shattered Church*, 27.

Hauerwas rightly reminds us of our need to reclaim the rich biblical category of *witness*. The root meaning of this word includes sacrifice equated with surrender. Any model rooted in more teaching must exhibit embodied, trustworthy ways that include emptying ourselves of control or fear. In this sense we witness to the fact that we trust the one who is called the Truth. Surprisingly, I have seen how this promotes a space to say more. Saying less and admitting our own limitations creates an openness for others to also be honest, and paradoxically more teaching can take place. This patience linked to humility is the kind of witnessing that leads to more teaching and in fact bypasses some of the resistance built up by those in a secular age.

Christians should strive to be witnesses where God has placed them. In fact, no one should be allowed to teach if they are not first of all committed to being witnesses of the new life the Bible speaks about. That means we consider what it means to be slow to speak and quick to practice fruitful dialogue that prioritizes listening well. This provides those in a secular age with an example of what Jesus did with his followers and those who struggled to believe. He called them to return to the mystery that God was teaching them new things that they did not anticipate. It is my hope that we will still believe that the Bible awakens us to this reality today. God has more to teach us than we can, at times, fully grasp in one hearing. Besides, a sensitive awareness is needed to see what God is doing in us and through us, as an essential aspect of how he wants us to teach others. In this way, the mystery of a transformed life, as spoken about in the Bible, converges with what is heard and seen.

THREE ATTITUDES FOR MORE TEACHING

In the Letter to the Hebrews, this idea is stated succinctly: "Remember your leaders, those who spoke to you the word of God. Consider the outcome of their way of life and *imitate their faith*."[13] A secular age tired of inauthentic personalities will continue to be suspicious of those who do not embody a life of integrity. Moreover, as people get serious about studying the Bible or attending church, they will also need those whose lives are worth imitating. Let's explore three attitudes that reveal daily dependence on God and can create space for more teaching.

---

13. Heb 13:7.

Less Telling, More Teaching

Humility: I am still learning

While people now have endless options to explore spirituality, the Bible speaks of how to grow and move past the general, fuzzy vibe of spirituality. That biblical alternative involves deeply rooted teaching. Those in a secular age should sense that how the Bible addresses spirituality is different than the other ideas they hear about spirituality. Here, it will be humility that distinguishes the kind of teaching that sets the Bible apart. While we can be confident about essential truths of the faith, we too are still learning. The God who Christians worship, as described in the Bible, is one who gives humans the room to learn and grow. In so doing he warns of pride that stifles that process. This is encompassed in the biblical image of a renewed mind.

Some of the teachings about God the Father, God the Son, and the living power of God the Holy Spirit are not easily understood without careful teaching. Yet, this essential Christian doctrine of the Trinity should always be approached with humility. The Bible reveals Jesus exemplifying the reality of this approach when he tells his own followers: "I still have many things to say to you, but you cannot bear them now."[14] Maybe we have forgotten that God, in his loving and gracious ways, is teaching us as he reforms and renews our perspectives. When pride takes root, I too can forget this at times.

Compassion: I feel your pain

Passio is the Latin word for suffering. In fact, it is from this word that we associate with "the passion" of Christ. It means the suffering of Jesus associated with Holy Week. Now think about it. What might com-*passio* mean? Maybe you got it. Compassion means to suffer *with* someone. Accordingly, I want to suggest that teaching is an approach that can be associated with the pain, change, unrest, and disorientation at the heart of our shifting secular age. It is an approach to teaching that says "you are not alone; I feel your pain" and "we can get through this together."

At times, I have seen that it is pain, and deep questions about suffering, that prepares those in a secular age to hear the Bible in new ways. These moments of vulnerability should be met with compassion. Thankfully we are not left on our own to figure this out. The Bible speaks of these issues

---

14. John 16:12.

and reminds us how Jesus found people who experienced his compassion as an important step to encountering his life-changing teaching.[15]

Joy: We are made for more than trends

The kind of teaching that I have been proposing will require that we guide those in a secular age beyond the doom and gloom narratives of this world. The good news is that more teaching should awaken more joy. People we meet in the Bible were able to process the pain of their situations while hearing of a new kind of hopefulness that Jesus' ways could offer. This kind of teaching does not ignore the sad challenges we all face, yet it points to something bigger, which the Bible describes as joy. Trends, likes, and viral videos will only continue to add to a fleeting sense of happiness that never materializes. While happiness is not bad, it is the right kind of teaching that unpacks the deeper gift the Bible calls joy.

When the Bible is heard as a gift linked with joy, something more formative happens. This comes at a time when teaching, learning, and a simple dialogue can too easily spiral into anger and vicious attacks. Joy, in this world, is in high demand. Imagine a kind of joy that is informed by a regular moments of learning from the Bible. I often think of the Fire Hawk, a bird that has been noted for spreading forest fires.[16] It picks up small branches with flames on them and drops it into other parts of the forest to start new fires. This is a fascinating practice linked to feeding, since during a fire all the little critters that run out of the forest become easy picking for this bird. It is a method of capitalizing on chaos and a secular age has monetized this approach. For many, the Bible is used in this way, and the kind of teaching that awakens joy remains a myth very few see embodied. Unfortunately, if we are not careful, we too can fall into this approach.

Here we offer those in a secular age a vision that includes more teaching that has anchored people for thousands of years. It has been a grounded truth through the pain of fluctuating events because it was the kind of teaching that stems from a timeless understanding of joy and not just the hype linked to the next viral craze. Put simply, we must find ways to reintroduce the Bible as God's gift offering us a joy that makes the love and grace of Jesus real still today. Only then will we begin to understand what Jesus meant when he said, "I have told you these things, so that in me you

---

15. John 4:1–42.
16. Greshko, "Why These Birds Carry Flames in Their Beaks."

may have peace. In this world you will have trouble. But take heart! I have overcome the world."[17]

AN EMPEROR'S FEAR OF GREAT TEACHERS

Earlier I mentioned the importance of learning from apostolic teachers. As the early church grew and expanded beyond the apostolic period a new wave of great teachers emerged. Thankfully, we have examples of how they reimagined teaching in a world where telling was interpreted as treason. In the fourth and fifth centuries tumultuous change was palpable. Soon, a new generation of Christian teachers found their vision for "more teaching" contested and rejected as dangerous by authorities of the Roman Empire. At the top of the ladder was the emperor himself. One emperor famously known as Julian the Apostate recognized the power of the Christian leaders' teachings and reacted to stop them.

Around 351, as he considered where and when Christians teaching might have influence, Julian noticed that Christian teachers had a particular influence in the way that they engaged with the ideas of the surrounding culture. Their skills in making connections with the story of Jesus while respecting the inherited cultural mores of the time was noticeable. Recognizing this, Emperor Julian decided to put a stop to these great teachers. He passed an edict that would inhibit those who were masters of teaching from continuing in this role.

What is particularly important to note for our secular context is that the edict stipulated that Christian teachers were not allowed to teach *non-Christian themes* linked to cultural influence of the day. Imagine that these Christian teachers were respected as teachers even when dealing with non-Christian topics. One esteemed historian of the period observed:

> [Julian] issued a formal edict excluding Christians from the teaching profession, a decision that was regarded as folly by pagans . . . and was resented by cultivated Christians like Gregory of Nazianzus who understood and loved the classical literature.

Hope you caught that. Even non-Christians recognized their skill in teaching.[18]

---

17. John 16:33.
18. Chadwick, *Early Church*, 176.

Emperor Julian was aware that the kind of wise and thoughtful teaching offered by these trusted Christian voices was being used to form new Christians. What made this approach to teaching "dangerous" to Julian was that it involved trusted Christian teachers/leaders who also knew the ancient classical philosophy of their time. Because these teachers had listened to the longings of their own culture, they could teach in such a way that honored the past, corrected errors, respected thoughtful ideas, and linked these diverse forms of wisdom to the uniqueness of Jesus.

It may come as a surprise, but those in a secular age will need more teaching that is similar to early church models. We live at a time when those with authority in schools or politics rarely meet Christians who embody the wisdom and teaching capacity to engage with different ideas. Less telling and more teaching requires that we both engage with those in a secular age and develop the kinds of future leaders that the church and the world need. This will always include a growing awareness of the cultural problems we face, our shortcomings, and differing worldviews. Moreover, it will have to be the kind of teaching that holds in tension what may be true and helpful among non-Christian thinkers. Christians throughout history have had to learn to cultivate these unique spaces for dialogue that consider shifts in learning and communication. This will shape a fresh vision of the Christian faith that will resonate with those in a secular age who have forgotten that Christians who love the Bible also appreciate literature, arts, music, and philosophy as aspects of being faithful to Jesus, whose truth extends beyond the pew.

Some of my first Christian experiences brought me face to face with an anti-intellectual stance toward everything in culture. This stance blinded me from seeing that the Bible emerged in a world of complex ideas. For too long I believed that you could just pull verses out of context and ignore the importance of loving God with all your heart *and mind*. Soon I was robbed of the great theological wisdom of the past and examples in history like the ones above. These anti-academic reactions made it difficult to know whom I could trust and how I could grow as a thoughtful leader who wanted to study the Bible as well as make a difference in the world. I wish I knew then of Apollinaris of Laodicea, who in the fourth century longed for people to know the Bible. To assist people with that "he published a version of [the] gospels and epistles in the form of Platonic dialogues."[19] If only I knew that

---

19. Chadwick, *Early Church*, 176.

you could both critique culture and learn from it as others before me had done.

This legacy is about looking for opportunities that involve more teaching while being aware of our secular age's default resistance to being told what to do or believe—less telling. Those who are shaped by a secular outlook at times consider Christians to be close-minded, since they are yet unaware of numerous example of diverse ways that the Bible has inspired Christians to love God with all their minds. In the next section we turn our attention to ways of reframing the authority of the Bible and its unique place in our lives. Biblical literacy must involve rethinking how we teach, by considering the framework of the listener.

I have heard numerous sermons justifying preaching that is all about telling. One person angrily approached me one day and said they were concerned that we were not preaching the Word at our church because I didn't just tell people exactly what to believe. He turned to this passage and read: "For the message of the cross is foolishness to those who are perishing, but to us who are being saved it is the power of God."[20] I told him that I believed with all my heart in the truth of that passage, but I did not think we are meant to miss the larger context. He had forgotten that Paul himself, at one time, thought the cross was foolishness as well. It was God's grace, coupled with faithful servants like Ananias, that helped Paul to accept what he once considered mere foolishness.

While Paul's story is special, the truth is that human foolishness remains a natural starting point for all of us. Our sin, our scars and struggles make us nervous about those who want to tell us what we should believe. This reality is our starting point as we present and share of God's goodness as found in the Bible. Accordingly, we remember that preaching the cross was never meant to just tell others that they are sinners without slowly teaching about how sin clouds our ability to understand and embrace God's goodness. This kind of teaching can be reclaimed as we return to the Bible.

SOLA NOT SOLO: RETURNING TO A PROPER UNDERSTANDING OF THE CENTRALITY OF SCRIPTURE

We know of another period in history when the Bible was reimagined in the face of cultural upheaval. It was the sixteenth century. It remains a movement equated with unrest in the church, culture, and politics. It is also

20. 1 Cor 1:18.

a time in our history that redefined learning and teaching forever. It was maybe one of the most formative times, when a shift from less telling to more teaching was initiated by a leader in the church. And it involved new ways to put the Bible back at the center of Christian maturity, discipleship, and reflections on culture. We call this the Reformation period.

The tagline *sola scriptura*, meaning Scripture alone, while not found in the Bible, remains helpful whenever we think of lessons related to the Bible and the Reformation period. When this tagline was first used, it spoke to concerns that the church, and some of its leaders, had moved away from a centrality of teaching the Bible to just telling. It also was a rallying cry for everyone, not just to a select few, to learn to hear, read, and embrace the good news that God speaks to us as we read the Bible and understand it in faithful congruence with the life and ministry of Jesus. Hence, *sola scriptura* was about correcting the long habit of just telling people about God without teaching them to grow, question, and see their lives as an important part of the church and its authority.[21]

The German Bible teacher Martin Luther remains one, but not the only, voice who sought to clarify the importance of the Bible for changing times. He reimagined a church where everyone would be exposed to the deeper teaching of the Bible in their own language. His was an admirable vision to re-center the Bible for dealing with all matters of faith, including the areas that called for reform in learning. Luther was aware, as are we, of the human inclination to make the Bible into something it was not meant to be. For some, this vision to return to the Bible soon got distorted and reverted to an approach of more telling than teaching. This happened by stretching the idea of "Scripture alone" to its unintended and problematic use as "Scripture *only*." Let's consider this subtle but serious difference.

The word *alone* meant that the Bible *alone* was to be the supreme gauge for matters of faith and doctrinal clarity. At no time was the goal to use the Bible and to suggest that it be the *only* book we could read or learn from. Today, we are left with many who interpret a deep love for the Bible to mean we can only really learn and read the Bible. This outlook is not correct for what was originally understood as *sola scriptura*, and it makes the Bible something it was never meant to be. It also assumes that telling people stories from the Bible is equivalent with teaching them to grow as they learn to study the Bible more faithfully. This requires tools like

---

21. While some of that is accurate, we know that young Roman Catholic monks like Martin Luther were in fact teaching the Bible. However, this often remained a priority only for academics.

commentaries and theological guides that assist us in studying the Bible well. Over the years the phrase "faith seeking understanding" has been helpful to remind us that those who love the Bible and embrace it as our authority can also continue to seek new and important understandings of it. Just *telling* people to read the Bible diminishes the richness of our faith, and the unique interplay between biblical truths, human experience, and the gift of scientific reasoning—and soon, added digital advancements.

The Bible alone was never meant to mean the Bible *only*. John Calvin, a leading sixteenth-century Reformer, once remarked: "The Holy Spirit had no intention to teach you astronomy."[22] A wise, and maybe cheeky, remark that God has provided diverse methods of learning, multiple streams of wisdom, that can teach us about the world and guide us in understanding the rightful and unique place of the Bible better. Most famously, in Acts 17 Paul himself acknowledged the helpful ideas of pagan poets that could awaken us to our human longing and the fullness of Jesus as the ultimate truth.[23]

This corrective lens will be essential for engaging with a secular age that is both educated and living through unprecedented expansions in knowledge. Affirming that the Bible stands above all other forms of learning as the most trusted and reliable source for understanding the good news of Jesus is, in no way, meant to minimize our need for other types of learning. Although the Bible *alone* carries unmatched authority for the truth about salvation in Christ alone, this salvation is meant to help discover the life we were meant to live. This is something those in a secular world are desperately in need of and it is founded on Jesus' command to "Go and *teach*, not go just go and tell."[24]

MORE TEACHING, LESS DIVISION

A few years ago, I regularly met with a young leader trying to grow and understand that their *telling* upbringing was no match for the complex world he was in. In one session together he remarked: "Why are there so many divisions of Christians?" Wow, that hit a nerve.

22. Calvin, *Commentaries*, Vol. 6, 184.

23. "God did this so that they would seek him and perhaps reach out for him and find him, though he is not far from any one of us. 'For in him we live and move and have our being.' As some of your own poets have said, 'We are his offspring.'" (Acts 17:27, 28 NIV)

24. Paraphrasing ideas in Matthew 28.

Not only did it bring me back to my early journey of faith and division in my home, but it prompted me to start paying closer attention to how my current teaching contributed to division in the church and the world. It is unquestionable that we live in an extremely divisive time. While sociologists and psychologists explore anthropological reasons for our present predicament, those in a secular age are deeply impacted by our present religious volatility. As this increases, I believe that God's plan is to use a more united church even when we don't always agree on certain matters. This is something the Bible addresses consistently.

The Bible takes these struggles seriously because when left unattended they cloud people's judgments and blur the hope of the gospel. One church in the Bible known for its painful division was found in the port city of Corinth. We learn that although the Corinthians, as Christians, should have matured and developed the ability to handle serious disagreement with wisdom, they acted in childish ways. Paul's rebuke did not involve blaming the world and surrounding culture. Instead, he wrote: "There is jealousy and dissension among you."[25] Jealousy and dissension in their own hearts was the problem. This included preference for one teacher over another, and envy between the teachers. Eventually, this lack of maturity spilled over and Paul, inspired by God, set out to address it.

I close with this little reminder that the Bible has much to teach us as we deal with similar issues today. It does so by pointing the finger at us, our churches, our approach to the Bible, and our responsibility to grow and mature as we deal with our culture. We must believe that God has what we need to help understand the shift from "less telling" to "more teaching" that minimizes divisiveness. When this happens, our gaze lifts off the negative patterns of our secular contexts to consider the sacred spaces of healing found in church communities. If we desire for the Bible to be read, prayed, and embraced as God's living words, we are wise to teach why different Christians can disagree yet respect and love each other.

It has been the goal of this chapter to shift our thinking from a common telling style of engagement that many Christians use when dealing with difficult struggles of our secular age. In fact, aggressive telling is a hallmark of our secular age and if we are not careful, we will find ourselves using the ways of world rather than the biblical examples of the one who has conquered the world. A confrontational approach will not lead to the kind of teaching that can withstand the pressures and suspicion of this age. Moreover, it will not form the kinds of leaders that can make a difference

---

25. 1 Cor 3:12.

Less Telling, More Teaching

now and into the future. This "more teaching" approach I am suggesting is more in line with what the ancient church called the work of catechesis, spiritual instruction in the mysteries of the faith that required wisdom, maturity, and patience. I hope Part 2 will add tangible markers for how we might reimagine a catechism for a secular age, one that addresses the special role of the Bible.

Recently I read a report that chess is now one of the fastest growing games among teenagers.[26] Yes, you heard me. Not only do they play video games, but YouTube sensations also have young people engaged in sitting, thinking, learning, and adapting as they watch online chess. Again, this is a great sign if we hope to equip and inspire a new generation with a fresh vision of the Bible that will not be a quick fix. Board games with the simpler moves we associate with checkers might have to make room for a new generation ready for added complexity and nuance. The resurgence of games like chess among young people may be one sign of many more to come. The movements between simple pieces that just move up and down are being reworked for the complexities of chess, which involves the multilayered movement of every piece. Even more, it is the game that teaches us that even the person with more pieces can lose.

Perhaps we have underestimated how much the next generation, formed in the throes of this secular age, can handle. In any event, they will ignore what we tell them if they do not trust that we have been listening before we teach. I am hopeful we can do now what others have done before us. We may be living at the cusp of new move of God's graciousness as signs of spiritual hunger fused with questions about global unrest and unimaginable suffering need our attention. More than ever, this will require us to embrace an encounter with the Spirit and a re-engagement with Scripture. When this happens, we will be confronted with the biblical admonition that our "speech [remain] gracious, seasoned with salt, so that you may know how you ought to answer each person."[27]

---

26. D'Anastasio, "Chess is Booming Among Teens."
27. Col 4:6.

PART 2

The Bible Heard as Living Words

"It is less important to ask a Christian what he or she believes about the Bible than it is to inquire what he or she does with it." –Lesslie Newbigin

NEW "LIVING" THINGS UNDER THE SUN

Nobel Prize-winner Nikolaas Tinbergen is known for his impressive research on deception. As part of one study on insect behavior he created fake female butterflies as a test to see if they could deceive male butterflies. As part of the experiment, his team carefully placed fake female butterflies, made to look like real ones, alongside real female ones. Then they watched the male butterflies. Soon a shocking pattern emerged during mating interactions. The male butterflies tended to be more attracted to the fake ones, which were more colorful than the real ones.

This type of research is part of a larger field of study known as simulation and behavior. In addition to being interesting, I think this area of study is reflective of our present world of deception and distortion, a growing conspiracy industry, and struggles to discern fake information. These ideas are now a natural part of our emerging secular age. We all know and sense how manipulation or distortion can make what is fake seem real and at times more appealing. There may not be a clean correlation between this prize-winning research and our human predicament, yet I think the human condition displays a propensity toward deception and confusion when left on its own. It is this reality that brings us back to our need for others, community, spiritual friendship, and mostly God's living words found in the Bible.

Our secular age will continue to reveal our lack of wisdom in discerning what is true, important, and real. For that reason, we need to reimagine the Bible since it is God's gift that brings us back to themes of truth and trust, which are paramount for how we interpret the Bible. At its core, this book has attempted to get honest about how we interpret and face challenges like this with head on. Part 2 of this book holds together the shifting realties of a secular age while addressing, with seriousness, the reality that many will have faulty views of the Bible. Also, we can't minimize how these misguided beliefs about the Bible can exacerbate the problems we face. Instead of seeing the Bible as living words that reveal God-given truth, many have fallen for the view that the Bible is made up of old and irrelevant suggestions. It is my hope that a renewed focus on the Bible will kick-start a conversation for both correcting these misguided ideas and speak about that Bible in ways that are more consistent with what the Bible actually is.

When we take the Bible seriously, we start to hear it and pay attention to where we have misunderstood it. Also, it has been my experience that it is the living words of the Bible, heard properly, that awaken the God-honoring courage to step out in faith and explore how we are meant to live. When this happens, we learn to love the Bible more, not less. We also desire to grow in understanding it because simplistic readings of the Bible do not correspond with the complexities of life we face. It is like hearing new sound frequencies that were there all along but never resonated clearly enough to hear them harmonize with what we sense in our hearts and minds.

When you hear the word *living*, what comes to mind? Maybe you imagine that first cry of a son or daughter. I still remember my son's first cry that came with piercing clarity about my new responsibilities as a dad. Perhaps *living* involves the scent of spring, where what was dormant is now showing new signs of life. In Part 2 of this book, I want to reaffirm and reimagine how our secular predicament requires that we return to speaking and teaching from the Bible in a way that touches numerous aspects of human existence and our need for a hopeful vision of what the future holds. You'll notice terms like *hope, purpose, truth,* and *trust*. No matter what shifts we face, God has created us with an ongoing hunger for congruency between our inner lives and our interactions with the world around us. This is why we all dislike any form of hypocrisy. Moreover, the good

Introduction to Part II

news is that our secular context has only magnified our human longing for what is real, authentic, and trustworthy.

With that in mind, each chapter in this section will explore how to read the Bible and understand its rich layers that accentuate its living words as God addressing our human longing to know who we are and who he created us to be.

For too long even those who have read the Bible have missed the joy-filled signs of new life. Take the popular passage from the book of Ecclesiastes stating that there is nothing new under the sun.[1] For years, I have heard people come back to it as a "catch-all" for ignoring change around us. Some preachers even minimize our shifting culture using the Bible. They remark: "Do not worry about the world; this is all old stuff we have seen before because 'there is nothing new under the sun.'"[2] Although this interpretation may make some feel better, it is not an accurate interpretation that aligns with what the rest of the Bible reveals and what those in a secular age need to hear.

Jesus, the eternal Son of God incarnate, is *a new thing under the sun*. A dead Messiah resurrected after three days as the cornerstone of our faith is *a new thing under the sun*.[3] The power that fell at Pentecost awakening the nations to the love of God for all people was a *new thing under the sun*. I think you get the point. We need to admit that there is a way of reading the Bible that devalues its living nature, pointing to the fact that there are new things being made known to us. The literary style of a book like Ecclesiastes is not meant to be taken literally or it would contradict all the other new things God does in the broader trajectory of the Bible, up to and through the New Testament. Sure, to God, there is nothing new under the sun, but for us, we may just be on the cusp of a fresh move of God, who might be calling us to welcome his surprises as we engage with a secular age.

As you read Part 2, I hope you sense that God continues to awaken you to curiosity, wonder, and even a form of doubt that is meant to reveal some of our deepest human longings. The struggles of our present secular context will require us to create new bridges of engagement that lead to safe spaces for people to ask for help. In fact, whenever we get serious about the Bible, we come face to face (or better, ear to ear) with the words of a *living and loving God*. While a secular age continues to morph and manipulate

---

1. Eccl 1:9.
2. Eccl 1:9.
3. 1 Cor 15.

and question what is real, I want to suggest that the time is right for us to return to the Bible with a fresh vision of hope and intrigue. As we do this, we can reframe with joy how the Bible addresses with accuracy and truthfulness our human struggles that have only been intensified by our secular age, not silenced.

In the Middle Ages, some castles had prisons known as oubliettes. If you need a mental image, just think of a hole in the ground. In French, the root word is *oublier,* which means "to forget." Prisoners placed in these chambers were meant to be forgotten and left to die. Too many people shaped by our shifting secular age are carrying deep feelings likened to those forgotten. They sense they are being forgotten by God, by the government, by the church, by their family. Moreover, they have distant ideas about the Bible that are fading, causing them to forget the hope that is available when the words of the Bible are embraced as living words for the life we are meant to live. My hope is that Part 2 of this book will provide some helpful moments of reawakening that will excite you about the life God created you to live. In so doing, it may become clearer than ever that you and I have not been forgotten or left on our own as we navigate issues in this secular age.

CHAPTER 4

From the Bible as a Manual to the Bible as a Compass

"The Bible held me rapt. The words stepped off the page and followed me home."[1] –Bono

"KEVIN, ARE YOU READING YOUR BIBLE?"

UBER-FAMOUS COMEDIAN KEVIN HART tells a story that captures the way the Bible is used and understood in our culture. Years ago, during an interview with Oprah Winfrey, he told a moving story about his mom that included the Bible. Following a difficult stretch without a job, he mentioned that he called his mom and hinted that he needed help to pay the rent. His mom said: "Kevin, are you reading your Bible? When you read your Bible, we will talk about the rent money." This happened on a few occasions and as Hart reveals, he confessed that reading the Bible was not a priority for him. In a moment of frustration, he said: "Yes, Mom, I'm reading my Bible, but what about the rent?" Finally, he shares how to his surprise, he found six months' worth of checks to cover his rent tucked into the Bible.[2]

For many, this story, now a viral video, is a powerful and emotional story that shapes how they engage or develop their views on the Bible. Left unattended, our culture shapes our thinking that fosters the kinds of beliefs that make the Bible a magical book with tips to get us through tough times in life. In my role as a pastor people have told me strange stories where they

---

1. Cosper, "Bono's Punk-Rock Rebellion," para. 28.
2. "Hard Lesson Kevin Hart's Mother Taught Him."

just open the Bible and put their finger on a verse and felt it was a sign just for them. Jokingly I've said, "Watch out for the one that says Judas hung himself." If you've made it this far in this book, you know this is no joke. Over the years, silly and sad approaches to the Bible have left me convinced that a secular age will both expose and add to the confusion.

Stories like that of Kevin Hart point to the urgency in rethinking a more robust way for understanding the Bible properly and reading it to explore how best to navigate our present secular circumstances. This chapter will address how easily people associate the Bible with a manual for life especially in moments of crisis. At first glance that sounds fine, but a deeper issue surfaces when we realize that we don't care about manuals. This image for the Bible is often linked to why people read the Bible so little. Instead, I want to propose a shift from the Bible as manual to the Bible as a compass that calls us to step into new and exciting moments where we can experience God's goodness and learn to trust him more.

The idea of a compass also resonates with a deep longing by those in a secular age direction and purpose in life. It has never been more important to reaffirm that the Bible, as living words, has much to say and teach on this issue. My hope is that we might think of fresh ways to draw people back to reading their Bibles from this different perspective. In so doing, they may recognize anew that our human longing to find fulfillment in our work, in our contribution to the world, and in cultivating a deep sense of purpose is informed by a loving God. It is my experience that when people start to see and understand the living words of the Bible in this way, they also grow in their commitment to read it with regularity.

The Bible does not use the image of a compass, as we would think about it in our modern context, but there are numerous passages about direction and decision-making. For instance, one I have often returned to for direction says: "Trust in the Lord with all your heart and lean not on your own understanding; in all your ways submit to him, and he will make your paths straight."[3] Maybe you know that feeling as well. It is that moment when you learn the Bible doesn't have a simple answer for you, and that God provides guideposts that may not make every path safe, but he does make the path straight and worth following.

I hope the diverse images we explore will stir hope in the good things that God offers us as we listen to and understand the Bible better. I have found myself stuck in my spiritual maturation because simplistic images,

---

3. Prov 3:5–6.

and shallow uses of the Bible, kept me from seeing the new things God was inviting me into. One of those hurdles stemmed from the idea of the Bible as a manual. Without realizing it, this created a stumbling block in my thinking and ongoing maturity. The Bible, when relegated to a type of manual, was something I thought was useful only when I had a problem. In a secular age, the Bible as a manual aligns with how Kevin Hart thought of the Bible. One turns to it as a last resort to help with a problem, hoping for a sign, yet never tasting the joy and discipline of reading it, with consistency, as living truth.

DOES GOD REALLY HAVE A PURPOSE FOR ME?

Imagine what happens if we reclaim the Bible's unique role for speaking into this human yearning for purpose and meaning. I have thought about this often since for years people have asked: "Does God *really* have a purpose for my life?" It is one of the most primitive human longings. It stems from a deeply vulnerable question: "Does it even matter that I am here?" Whenever I am with people wondering about this I ask: "Are you reading your Bible to see how God guided others working through a similar question?"

For many, the puzzled looks lead to shock because they rarely read the Bible, assuming it has nothing to say to them. While they might never say it, they see the Bible as a manual that you might check when you have problems, rather than living words that provide ongoing lessons with directional insights that lead to a fulfilled life. Moreover, few have even read enough of the Bible to know that it does not shy away from people who also ignored their purpose in life and the pain that ensued when this gift of participating in God's good plans was ignored.

When these assumptions about the Bible are left unattended, those in a secular age turn to other options to address their human longings for purpose. Consequently, they miss the gift of the Bible and the rich truth it provides. For that reason, I think it will help to reposition our view of the Bible as compass rather than a manual. This provides a broader and more expansive image that implies that God not only cares about our struggles, but also thrusts us into surprising adventures to dream, accomplish, and discern new things he has set in advance for us to do. Surely, a God who gives life purpose, and a God who says *go* and make disciples, has left us insights for how to discover and pursue his ways with wisdom.

While secular culture seems to be creating new space for spiritual conversations, questions about purpose create room to move past the generic "I believe in God" kind of talk to "If God still speaks, how do we learn to hear him?" During my years as a university chaplain, I encountered the anxiety students felt around the whole area of the Bible and the idea of purpose. Clouded by strange ideas related to *God's will for my life*, many had subconsciously internalized a view of the Bible that had very little to offer as they tried to figure out the life they were meant to live. This only added to the many voices pressuring them to figure out a career. In that setting, young people who had dreams and goals also wanted to honor God with their lives. Sadly, their skewed outlook of the Bible led them to rarely read it for the kind direction it offers.

At a time when those in a secular culture are searching for clarity through esoteric vision quests and the use of shamans and clairvoyants, we are wise to reaffirm the gift of the Bible that points to a God who speaks and leads us in his ways. In this sense, sharing about *how* the Bible guides us will land on open ears and seeking hearts and minds. For that to happen, we must adjust to the Bible as so much more than just a manual with spiritual tips that might get us out of a jam. Instead, I want to explore what it means to hear the biblical message in a way that makes directional sense to our lives, and explore the deep gift of a life lived with purpose.

PURPOSE BETWEEN MODERN AND POSTMODERN

The French philosopher Rémi Brague asks: "Is it good that you are here?" to confront a certain nihilistic malaise associated with today's secular culture.[4] Suicide, depression, and other cultural factors reveal a new kind of despair that point to a loss of purpose for many people. Brague's question is both rhetorical and reflective. Although the answer is "yes," we should add that it is also important for us *to know why* we are here and that being here, on this planet, at this very time in history, matters. This is what it means to embrace our place and purpose. In Part 1, we explored the old narratives about a secular culture. One aspect involved an approach that thought that arguments defending the existence of God were what we needed. However, while those may be interesting, we have missed that other important apologetic perspective will require we also address, "Is God good?" A fresh reading of the Bible will help us with this.

4. Brague, *Curing Mad Truths*.

From the Bible as a Manual to the Bible as a Compass

What I have noticed is that many people who are shaped by the values of a secular culture are leaning toward discussions related to goodness rather than what is true.[5] In a world devoid of hope, the possibility of a good God who loves us is worth exploring. As one student once asked, "Is the Christian story good for humanity?" Do the doctrines we believe point to a hopeful view of the future? Some Christian traditions have read the Bible solely through the lens of things just being bad and only getting worse. Those in a secular age will find this very confusing. While there is some wise biblical warning about the bleak challenges of this world, we may need to reclaim a more balanced tension. When we read the Bible properly, bad and good are always understood in light of Jesus' authority and his kingdom unfolding on earth as it is in heaven. This even informs how Jesus taught us to pray.[6]

A modern view of the world suggested that we are here by a mechanistic fluke of nature. What that meant is that our lives had no purpose unless we produced something to give ourselves worth. There was no larger story that we embraced that helped us discover our true purpose within God's good plans for us. It is becoming clearer that this so-called modern, Enlightenment worldview wasn't that enlightening or encouraging. It missed the concerns for goodness, meaning, and purposefulness at the core of human nature. Those who bought into this modern outlook often read the Bible through that filter. That means that they soon found themselves increasingly trapped in a cycle where discernment in decision-making seems unimportant since things are really up to chance and luck.

For example, this kind of sloppy determinism hears passages like "In their hearts humans plan their course but the Lord establishes their steps"[7] to mean we should make no plans since God has already *controlled* our steps. However, a different, and more faithful, reading of this verse recognizes the larger story of the Bible, which invites us to plan, dream, and prepare for a life of purpose. This includes reflecting on what God is calling us to change or what matters to surrender to his guiding wisdom.

We are living through a transition where the modern outlook proposed above is morphing in a postmodern one. Instead of everything being predetermined, our secular age is one of disruption, change, and endless

---

5. I think reimagining Christian apologetic should move toward questions about goodness and how that links to issues of ultimate truth. Just *starting* with ideas about "Truth" is often interpreted as arrogant by those in our secular age.

6. "May God's will be done on Earth as it is in Heaven" (Matt 6:10).

7. Prov 16:9.

possibilities—a form of intellectual whiplash. All along we are left with our Bible, trying to encourage engagement with what God is doing no matter the changes around us. This is the important work that awaits as we move from a static manual lens of the Bible that minimizes our humanity, to a compass image that awakens us to the importance of our voice, our vision, and our part in God's redemptive plans. We have never been so knowledgeable about so many things and yet so hungry to know why we long to see our lives, our communities, our cities, and our churches shaped by God's redemptive hope.

I tend to be cautiously optimistic that what is coming after the modern world will provide spaces for us to reimagine the gift of the Bible in new ways. While some use the term *postmodern* as solely negative, it is not that simple. Both modern and postmodern periods have strengths and weaknesses. Accordingly, what will be required is a new perspective that acknowledges that fewer and fewer people know that the Bible sheds light on the types of human issues that really matter to us. Further, the Bible addresses the human uncertainties we feel as we learn to find our purpose.

One ancient prayer states: "Lord, teach us to number our days that we may gain a heart of wisdom."[8] This short prayer orients our mind to remember that God has a way of teaching us to see our lives as both significant and temporary. Without sounding mean, "numbering one's days" is a nice way of saying "you and I are going to die." An aimless life forgets this and thus ignores the careful reflection needed to make decisions related to our purpose. However, when we approach that Bible as a compass that can guide and direct us, we become more intentional about our choices. Soon, we find God prompting us as we also consider the consequences of our decision. The biblical truth about numbering our days alerts us to the fact that not everything matters in the same way.

If we think about it just a little deeper, "purpose" is not only the end goal or destination of life. Instead, it is an ongoing recalculation and recalibration of what makes life meaningful. This requires courage to say no when our decisions may not honor God or align our lives with purpose. I wish I had understood this biblical principle sooner. For years I, like many, learned about the Bible in a way that did not provide wisdom for daily life situations. Hence, I missed how even small decisions in my life were steps to teach me to embrace the larger story of the Bible. Here again, I think that when the Bible is seen as a manual we can pull random verses out of

---

8. Ps 90:12.

From the Bible as a Manual to the Bible as a Compass

context, clinging to detached stories in the New Testament and not seeing their important connection to the larger story God is writing with our lives, meant to bring him glory. I did not understand that the Bible was not meant to be a book on a shelf to revisit at one's leisure but so much more than that. A helpful correction was to view the Bible as a compass that offers ongoing direction.

PRACTICES OF LIVING WITH PURPOSE

Manuals are not bad; however, this image creates hurdles when it becomes a dominant way of understanding the Bible. One of the reasons the view of the Bible as manual sticks is that it is both simple and oriented toward private reading of the Bible. While the Bible speaks to us in personal ways, its reading is not meant to be seen as solely a private affair. Those shaped by a secular age, even when they start to read the Bible, will default to this private approach. Just like the manual in my car's glove box, the Bible is then used as a book I glance through when the check engine of life light comes on. I get an update, do a reset, and then I put the manual away. I hope you see how the Bible is anything but a manual.

I still remember when I fell for this manual idea of the Bible. It soon detached my thinking from the larger story of the Christian faith. Important connections to our rich Christian history that I have referred to in this book were often ignored. For instance, I did not realize that before the Bible was put into written form, the earliest followers of Jesus *heard* and recognized and embraced Jesus' message, itself carrying a particular kind of *living* truth in and for a community. This living experience, attached to daily purpose, was formed around the practice of gathering as the church, eating together, praying together, and practicing key living activities in line with the larger purpose of life that always included others.

The *living* part was linked to the fact that Jesus had himself come and walked as a living person who said things about God that resonated at the deepest level of our humanity. For example, the Bible comments about a crowd who "were amazed at his teaching, because he taught as one who had authority, and not as their teachers of the law."[9] The word *authority* here does not mean to act bossy or in charge, but describes the way the living words of Jesus fit, made sense of, and gave new meaning to their questions in a way that other teachers did not. It might help to remember that our

9. Matt 7:28–29.

English word *author* is in the word *authority*. In that way, Jesus' authority brought together ideas that only "the author" would know.[10]

What Jesus did was reconnect their questions to the larger story of Israel in the Old Testament while reorienting them to something even bigger. Additionally, he helped them to see that their purpose was being reshaped to prepare them for new things that were emerging. Anchored in this truth, Jesus left us living practices that the Bible records as most essential. These living practices are linked to God's larger and ongoing purposes unfolding in our midst. God knew we would need living practices to counter the discouraging and dead ways of our broken world. One of the most sacred practices that points to the past as well as the future is called communion, or, as the Greek word states, *eucharisteo*—a word that means thanksgiving.

Paul, who wrote many of the books in the New Testament, recalls the oral nature of this practice when he writes to those in Corinth. Surprisingly, he talks about this living practice as an anchor to each other and to God's larger purpose. If you remember from a previous chapter, the church in Corinth was dealing with many divisions and conflicts. Hear what Paul writes:

> For I received from the Lord what I also passed on to you: The Lord Jesus, on the night he was betrayed, took bread, and when he had given thanks, he broke it and said, "This is my body, which is for you; do this in remembrance of me." In the same way, after supper he took the cup, saying, "This cup is the new covenant in my blood; do this, whenever you drink it, in remembrance of me." For whenever you eat this bread and drink this cup, you proclaim the Lord's death until he comes.[11]

This is a remarkable passage when we stop to remember that Paul was *not* there on the night when Jesus was betrayed. He would have had no firsthand idea of the details of Judas's betrayal and the shocking ways Jesus redefined the Passover forever. Paul would *not* have experienced Jesus washing his disciples' feet and the raw realties of carrying the cross. All this means is that Paul is repeating a *living*, ongoing practice in the life of the church, one that Jesus himself told him about.

In order to shift people's view of the Bible we must find ways to help them hear it and practice what it says. When the Bible is heard properly, it directs us to understand the past as we prepare for the new things coming

---

10. This does not mean that all the other teachers during the time of Jesus were bad.
11. 1 Cor 11:23–26.

From the Bible as a Manual to the Bible as a Compass

in the future. In fact, if you read the passage again, you'll see that. We remember what Jesus did as we await the joy of when Jesus returns. This is anything but static or mundane information many in a secular culture might equate with dead rituals for religious types. Communion, community, and a commitment to hearing the Bible are meant to awaken us to our place in the God-glorifying story.

The Bible offers us a living, moving, and adventurous life that refines our purpose in ways that will often surprise us. However, when the Bible is perceived as a manual, the larger vision it calls us into is demoted and a lively faith in Jesus is soon understood as boring, safe, and predictable. This often confirms and fits the suspicions of many in secular culture. Again, one of the best ways to move beyond seeing the Bible in this way is to read it, hear it, and step into a deep appreciation of living practices that point to the good things God is still accomplishing today.

When we understand this aspect of our faith, Bible reading is embraced as a living practice meant to address our need to live a life of purpose. Here is a biblical image that is linked to the idea of a compass, that directs and moves us. We read: "The word of God is alive and active."[12] When these words were first uttered, the whole Bible in the way we have it today was not yet available. Thus, one of the active things that God was doing was bringing his word, the Bible, together in a way that would consistently point us to Jesus, the living *Word* in our midst.

To modern thinkers, spoiled by the luxury of an endless supply of books, it can be a challenge to see the Bible and the words in it as living and active. When my kids were younger, they watched a movie called *Night at the Museum*. They were hooked on the idea that old and supposedly silent things in the museum could come to life at night. In some ways, the Bible involves an imaginative framework to see the words, and the stories, even the old stories, teeming with living truth that can help us as we explore life's purpose. The oral, living, and transforming truth made sense to the earliest followers of Jesus since it was heard as living, and then practiced as living.

The living words of the Bible were literally living and flowing out of the mouth of Jesus and passed on by ongoing interactions with his followers. In fact, that's one of the reasons we have four retellings of the same moments of the ministry of Jesus in the four Gospels. The audience, the authors, and the work of a living God embraced the subtle changes and nuances in the same story. With a manual view of the Bible, differences are

---

12. Heb 4:12.

seen as deficiencies that imply weakness or dishonesty. When we let go of such a simple manual image of the Bible, we realize that a compass and its ability to guide and adjust based on where one is standing becomes more helpful.

THE BIBLE AND THE GOD WHO HAS PURPOSES.

When the Bible is relegated to a type of manual we remain in control. In this sense, we decide to only read it when or if it suits us. Most commonly, we just look up something when we feel stuck, afraid, or have a problem to resolve. A few days ago, someone contacted me for my thoughts on the solar eclipse that they believed was connected to the end times. They asked where the Bible talked about these issues since they were nervous about what this could mean. The fact that they did not attend church or have any desire to grow in the larger purposes of God. This was not even something they recognized as an issue.

Partly because I did not say it directly, it took some time to explain how problematic it was to approach reading the Bible as a manual due to fear. This is a common challenge in churches that also spills over to influence those who are unsure about faith, the Bible, and the role of the church. Some even get frustrated that they cannot find a simple list of how-to items related to navigating marriage conflicts, the end times, dating, or some easy steps for when to quit your job, etc. Hence, the rich interplay between living community, living words, and living truth as found in the Bible are overshadowed by a shallow and self-serving manual mindset. Soon, the way the Bible situates our longing for purpose in God's larger purposes never takes root.

An important corrective to the manual outlook requires that we revisit the biblical image of a God who himself has purposes. This means he is moving, working, and calling people to follow, to change, to surrender, and to live life fully aware of his purposes. The Bible as a manual makes me the center. The Bible as a compass disorients us enough to keep us sensitive to God's leading, which often guides us beyond our comfort zone.

Recalling the exodus, the Bible offers a prayer that reads: "Your path led through the sea, your way through the mighty waters, though your footprints were not seen. You led your people like a flock by the hand of Moses and Aaron."[13] I hope you hear the living truth in that prayer. Finding our

---

13. Ps 77:19–20.

place in God's purposes is not that easy. In fact, the process of learning to listen to God in difficult moments is God's way of developing us to trust him as we discover the life we were meant to live. Even Moses felt lost or unsure at times, yet he kept moving forward in faith. If such great giants of our faith needed help to make sense of the purposes of God, we should not be surprised when we struggle to fully discern with ease what God has in store for our lives.

For me, Moses remains the greatest example of how we wrestle with God as part of submitting to God's purposes. As a pastor and a parent this passage has a special place in my maturity and growth. I often remind myself that Moses is discerning the ways of God not just for himself but for the people he is leading. Maybe you will feel this as a mom or dad. Or maybe you are leading a company and feel that a decision you make has huge implications for others who work for you. God cares about how our choices impact others. For that reason, the Bible must remain our guiding compass even if all we can do is take is one step forward and then pause and pray.

While God has a purpose for us, there is something special about the way the Bible addresses the theme of purpose. This includes a surprising awareness that God himself has plans and purposes. Yes, this is formative as we let the Bible play a more central role in our lives. In a secular culture themes associated with spirituality often only address *our* human desire to discover *our* purposes. While this is a natural starting point, as we mature in our love for God we seek to embrace his purposes, not just our own. Daily, we must confess with the biblical writer who admits: "'For my thoughts are not your thoughts, neither are your ways my ways,' declares the Lord. 'As the heavens are higher than the earth, so are my ways higher than your ways and my thoughts than your thoughts.'"[14] When we do not learn this, we confuse our desires with God's direction. No one is fully privy to God's thoughts, but his loving guidance provides direction as we trust him. With the image of a compass in mind, consider these four principal reference points.

COMPASS POINTS: FOUR WAYS THAT POINT TO GOD'S PURPOSES

The word *telos* is used by theologians to capture the overarching purposes of God and how they are expressed in the Bible. *Telos* is a directional word

14. Isa 55:8–9 (NIV).

that makes sense when you see the Bible as a compass. It makes even more sense if we remember we are *followers* in the way of Jesus. While some in our culture may fuse this idea with the theme of progress, the Bible reminds us that "progress" without a larger sense of purpose and responsibility can lead to unethical situations. To keep us grounded, the Bible as a compass also has a strong magnetic pull meant to keep drawing us back to a Christ-centered way of life. This invisible force is an illuminating love that reveals that our lives matter, and what we do with them can and should fit into God's larger purposes.

Over the years, I have thought of the north, south, east, and west directions on a compass as a grid for hearing the Bible and making choices. In so doing, I have also prayed that God would help me improve my sensitivity to his leading. What I have found helpful about this is that these four directional lenses draw on patience and perseverance as key characteristics related to a biblical view of purpose. Life, and the choices we make, are not meant to always follow straight lines. We fail, we fumble, we forget, and God remains faithful. In this way, the Bible is always sensitively reminding us that we are human. That means we can slow down for rest and reflection as part of developing a better sense of God's purposes and ours. A compass has a fixed true north. For us, that is Jesus, the eternal and living Word of God. He is gracious with us as he was with his earliest followers. Let's consider Matthew, the tax collector, as an example.

GOD'S PURPOSE: SO MUCH MORE THAN A DESTINATION

Many stories in the Bible warn of how we might pursue a shallow life when purpose is defined only by power and prosperity. Matthew, or Levi, provides us with just one example that links purpose to a disordered focus on profit and even a sense of prestige. He was a tax collector whose life aligned with an oppressive government.[15] We don't get to see his heart, but something was not right and Jesus could tell. Soon enough, Jesus redefined and reawakened him to a different understanding of purpose.

We do not have all the details of how Matthew moved on from being a tax collector and the consequences that ensued. But the Bible does make clear that Matthew left his old life and followed Jesus. I wonder what the first conversation with his family was like? Did they downsize their house?

15. Matt 9:9–13.

Did Jesus ask him to go make things right with people he might have taken advantage of? The Bible, in the Gospel attributed to Matthew, records key moments that led to this Jewish tax collector stepping out to follow Jesus. Just as he did with Matthew, Jesus is still calling people to step out into a new direction with a new sense of purpose that may not be easy, but will definitely be worth it.

Matthew's old purpose was transformed to fit God's purposes. His worst mistakes were transformed for a more restorative way of living. I think of many who are engulfed by the complexities of our secular age and whose lives have been solely focused on wealth, with priorities detached from God's purposes. I believe they would find unique affinity with Matthew's story. They, like Matthew, may be ready to surrender to a bigger and more fulfilling purpose for their lives. When God corrects our simplistic view of the Bible, he also reworks our shallow views of what we once believed about his purposes.

Below is a simple guide to engage with the Bible by paying attention to the natural human need for focus. We each wonder about what's going on beyond this world. If there is a God, does he care and is he speaking? I call this an upward direction that entails worship. Then we consider the downward direction, the space of surrender and serving others. God's purpose always involves this. Depending on where we are standing, we all know we need to look backward, for how past decisions or regrets have formed us. We are "historied" beings, and our past impacts us. Lastly, there is the forward direction. Here we want to know that we can move into the future with hope. Each of these directional markers should play a part in how we read the Bible and understand the way it is meant to guide us.

North: Upward Direction and Understanding Worship

Worship is a multidimensional term that encompasses all of life. However, the gathering of Christians on the day forever associated with the resurrection of Jesus is paramount for thinking about the purpose of our lives. In an "upward" way we consistently need moments when we turn our face and hands upward with and among God's people. The world around us needs to know that God has left us a rhythm of rest and worship that is intricately linked to his creative purposes. If we had time, we might consider sabbath as the most common practice related to this upward expression. God's transforming work is not a private thing, but a communal reality. For the early Christians, the Bible was always heard in this upward communal context. Consider such passages as this: "After you have read this letter, pass it on to the church at Laodicea so they can read it, too. And you should read the letter I wrote to them."[16] Before we move in other directions, the Bible as a compass always directs us to consider the importance of worship.

South: Downward Direction and Understanding Serving

Mistaking the Bible for a manual makes us believe that the Bible is primarily about how we live an accomplished life. Here, categories such as failing or succeeding, winning or losing, become the way we define our significance. The more we lean on the compass nature of the Bible, the more freeing it is. Also, we learn that if God wanted a world dominated by efficiency, he would have accomplished his purpose by using angels instead of humans. Conversely, the Bible reveals a God who invites humans like me and you to serve others. Descent is the way of the gospel. This is a key direction that Jesus himself modeled in fulfilling God the Father's purposes. How foolish to think it would not play a part in our lives. In fact, our lives are much more purposeful when we serve and help others. Even some of the most recent scientific research is revealing that.

East: Backward Direction and Understanding Our Past

Let's return to Matthew. His past required healing. I believe that the Bible records his story for us to remember that God uses people with a messy past. I think our past contains helpful keys that either block or unlock how we read and understand the Bible. More importantly, when we let God's grace flow from the pages of the text, we hear that even our worst mistakes do not disqualify us from playing a part in his larger redemptive purposes. A secular culture shaped by shame and failure is dying for this message of hope and healing. As we reconnect people with the Bible and the living truth it offers, those in a secular culture who struggle alone through mishaps are offered a different way of defining where they have come from and where they are going.

---

16. Col 4:16.

FROM THE BIBLE AS A MANUAL TO THE BIBLE AS A COMPASS

West: Forward Direction and Understanding Our Future

A healthier understanding of our past makes conversation about the future exciting. Here we experience the Bible's offer of hope. Medical leaders in the US have noted: "Despite substantial prevention efforts, between 1999 and 2017, suicide and nonfatal self-injury rates have experienced unprecedented increases across the United States—as well as in many other countries in the world."[17] While there are numerous factors for such discouraging news, a secular culture may be more open than ever to hearing how the Bible inspires us to dream about a more hopeful future. Imagine what would happen if those overwhelmed by the stress and anxiety found a renewed sense of purpose informed by the Bible—God's guiding presence and living words that awaken a joy in knowing our lives are part of a purposeful story.

HOLY SPIRIT: A GOD WHO DIRECTS WITHOUT DICTATING

Whenever you talk about the Bible, you can't go too far without talking about the Holy Spirit. One reason for this is that the Bible tells us that it was the Holy Spirit that *inspired* the biblical authors. That same Holy Spirit also makes the words of the Bible come alive as living words so that we hear them and see their importance for a life with purpose. Because of sloppy and even dangerous uses of the Bible, we have a generation that has dismissed the Bible as irrelevant.

The image of a compass creates room to explore how the Holy Spirit provides directional wisdom without dictating. It reminds us that God provides direction, but he doesn't dictate every step we take in life. This can be such a liberating feeling, one that celebrates the diversity of our faith journeys yet keeps us focused on God's larger narrative. You and I might make very different decisions about life, or leadership, and yet still feel at peace with where God has placed us. When I was younger, I wanted a God who dictated what I should do at every turn. It made me feel like I could wash my hands when things went wrong, thinking "Oh, it was God's will." I imagined a Bible with index entries like:

"Easy steps for managing family conflict."

---

17. Martinez-Ales et al., "Why Are Suicide Rates Increasing in the United States," lines 2–4.

"Five clear signs it's time to quit your job."

"How to deal with annoying in-laws."

"Always knowing which school to attend."

In our modern world, addicted to fast and efficient steps, we may feel some frustration with a Bible that invites us into a slower, more reflective way of living. The Bible does this by correcting when the ways of the world distort the way we are meant to read and hear God's voice addressing us. Instead, with care, attention, and discipline, we are called to learn to read the Bible slowly and get acquainted with the fact that it is a totally different kind of book. Yes, it is nothing like a manual. God's purposes are such that the biblical writers were inspired by the Holy Spirit not to impart a manual type of knowledge to us. More importantly, it pleased God to let us make a range of choices by following his direction without the pressure of dictation for every decision. Here we are free to learn and even change our mind as part of our maturity. We all know that if healthy parents want healthy kids, they create room for them to make choices. In this light, why would we think that God doesn't offer a similar approach for how he deals with us as his children?

One reason the Bible does not always offer a strict directive approach for every choice is that the Bible is meant to transcend any culture and time. It speaks of what people did at one time in history, but is still addressing us at this very moment in time. Manuals are books with basic information about a product we bought. Thus, they are linked to a particular time and a particular product. When we throw out the item, the manual becomes obsolete. The Bible is not like that. Instead, the Bible is an invitation into a life-altering journey to be embraced as an unpredictable adventure held together under a vision of the purposes of God. A secular culture has caused many to wonder and even doubt the Bible, suggesting that it is a manual that isn't worth reading with regularity. Those who are taught to see the Bible as a manual soon experience an inevitable frustration when the Bible does not address issues in a "fix-my-problem" kind of guide.

C. S. Lewis rightly observes: "[Jesus] hardly ever gave a straight answer to a straight question. He will not be, in the way we want, 'pinned down.' The attempt is . . . like trying to bottle a sunbeam."[18] Remember, the bigger picture is to see our lives, our decisions, and our desires continually being realigned to fit God's larger purposes. This, I believe, will be a new

---

18. Lewis, *C. S. Lewis Treasury*, 403.

and welcomed insight for those exhausted by a secular culture. It means that we can face the ups and downs of life with confidence, knowing that God's larger purposes are in no way weakened by a our messy world or our mistakes. God's desire has always been to have us reunited, in deeply loving union, with himself, and he accomplishes this in the daily, even hourly ways as he reminds us of our purposes and his.

This outlook requires trusting the Holy Spirit and moving beyond seeing the Bible as a manual to just resolve problems. It is instead meant to cultivate a living relationship with the living God. This ongoing work of the Holy Spirit reveals God's gift of direction without dictating as we explore the life we were meant to live. Imagine how profound this revelation will be to a generation that doesn't want to be told what to do.[19] They will learn of a God who provides guidelines but does not need to always just tell us what to do to remain sovereign. While his parameters are firm, how we live within them is how we discover the life we were meant to live.

A COMPASS: A GOD WHO IS IN CONTROL WITHOUT BEING CONTROLLING

I was almost eighteen years old when I first heard this idea of the Bible as a manual for my life. Unexpectedly, a friend invited me to a Christian youth retreat. I had never been to a gathering like this. It was encouraging to see other young people who wanted to make sense of life and serve God together. As part of the gathering the preacher repeatedly stated: "The Bible is the only manual you will need in life." I was young and wanted to grow in my understanding of the Bible but didn't realize how unrealistic and even problematic it would be to see the Bible as a manual.

If we hope to develop a more robust view of the Bible we must correct such simplistic ideas while considering the shifts of our secular age. That means we must model the joy and freedom to learn, make choices, and make mistakes, realizing that this does not necessarily imply we are being sinful or disobedient. All of this is a natural and human part of exploring our desire for purpose within God's larger plan. Allowing us to find our purpose, grow in it, requires a vision of the Bible that operates like a compass. It's our responsibility to make room to discuss, discern, and respond to the challenges of this age with wisdom.

---

19. See chapter 3.

Embracing the Bible as living words, with a compass in mind, can help inspire and create new paths of learning to trust God. *Cartographer* is the fancy word for one who makes maps. In a Google Maps world, with directions to any part of the globe at our fingertips, we can lose sight of how those in the Bible depended on the mapping of new lands, marking off dangers—and opportunities. If the Bible and its stories are heard and interpreted properly, they call us to pay attention to our next steps and our need to trust God, even when the whole map, revealing the exact decision to make, is not clear. It a part of our purpose in life to step out in faith.

Maps not only reveal covered terrain, but they also point to untraveled spaces. One of the most amazing video games of this past era is called *The Legend of Zelda: Breath of the Wild*. I have spent time watching my kids play it and have been drawn to its beauty, its creativity, and the endless imaginative possibilities. One cool feature of the game is linked to a richer reading of the Bible, as we have been exploring in this chapter.

When you begin the game you are given a map; however, it is mostly blank except for the place where you are standing. All you have are compass settings. When Link, the main character, begins to walk, the area he steps into appears on the map. Shockingly, one is aware of a vast territory for the whole game, yet you can only really see it by exploring it. Moreover, the goals and purposes of the game become more clear as more of the map is revealed. A compass provides direction, and only by moving in a particular direction are more details revealed. When I began to see the Bible as a gift that is meant to be read in a similar way, it set me free, and it inspired me to read it and see new ways God was encouraging me to step out in faith. I didn't have to wait for a secret sign or the exact answer to a prayer. Instead a sense of freedom slowly corrected a paralyzing fear that every decision needed exact clarity, and that any failure would be a sign of my lack of faith.

All of this required that I stop seeing the Bible as a manual. As part of this chapter, I've offered some warnings that may help us think about a new way forward while staying aware of the present issues of our secular age. It is my hope that our human longing to live with purpose will be more and more rooted in a rich understanding of the Bible. When we read the Bible properly, we get better at discerning how God guides and strengthens us, long after we have found the right job, or discovered a fulfilling career. When this happens, we begin to experience a fresh appreciation for how God speaks through the words of the Bible with consistency, even when we do not have a problem we need him to fix.

CHAPTER 5

From the Bible as a Textbook to the Bible as Inexhaustible Treasure

"I still have many things to say to you, but you cannot bear them now." –Jesus

"PEOPLE OF THE BOOK" AND OTHER RELIGIONS

"We are people of the Book" is a common phrase that Christians use to encourage others to get serious about the Bible. Unfortunately, it rarely leads to people reading the Bible more consistently. In a secular age it also creates a particular hurdle due to the conflicts associated with religious pluralism. I remember sitting down with a young adult studying world religions. She was fascinated with the ways people explore and express their views about the divine. As we chatted, she asked, "Don't other religious communities care about their sacred writings like Christians?" After a pause, she added, "Jews and Muslims have their own religious writings and care about following what is in their *books*. Are they not people of the Book as well?"

All her questions fit perfectly into the secular age we are trying to understand. They involve diverse perspectives, curiosity about differing views, and certain attitudes or beliefs that come across as arrogant. We cannot ignore that questions like this will require a deeper understanding of both the Bible and our faith. This kind of curiosity is related to spiritual longings that include a distrust toward exclusive truth claims that minimize a pluralistic mindset. Christians have, from the earliest days of the faith, had to find ways to respect others even when they disagreed with them. I still remember the earliest outline for this book took shape as I jotted down notes after my discussion with the young girl described above. Since then, these types of questions have only intensified both in the church and broader culture. For that reason, I want this book to be a tool as you consider the challenges of our present context that will involve ongoing dialogue with those in this secular age. As part of these dialogues, we will have to find ways to explore new language to reimagine the Bible and the wisdom it offers.

In this chapter, we will explore another image for thinking more deeply about Bible. As we revisit old categories, we also become aware of new ways to speak of the Bible—ways that resonates with those in a secular age. In so doing, we pray they would understand, read, and appreciate the uniqueness of the Bible. Moreover, this helps model respect towards those who hold different beliefs about faith, religion, and the Bible, which is a value many in a secular age are attuned to. One passage from the Bible commands: "In your hearts revere Christ as Lord. Always be prepared to give an answer to everyone who asks you to give the reason for the hope that you have. But do this with gentleness and respect."[1] I should add that the respect we are called to exhibit is not something that will always be reciprocated. Nevertheless, it remains a defining characteristic of those who want to obey the teachings of the Bible.

Over the years, I have had to learn how to apply this passage as a leader planting a church. In so doing, I became more sympathetic to the fact that a secular age is in some ways similar to that of the first century in which the Christian Bible came together. A similarity is a pluralistic world frothing with diverse forms of wisdom. In this regard, I believe people are open to exploring the *unique* wisdom that can be uncovered as we delve more into the idea of the Bible as living and reliable treasure of truth. However, one difference between our context and that of the first century is that many people are haunted by horrible things done by many who claimed to be Christians and yet didn't embody the wisdom of the Bible. This is our plight. We can never recreate the "clean slate" of the pre-Christian world. Ours is a post-Christian reality.

It is my belief that we need *more* space to explore the plurality of beliefs. Years ago a bumper stick many started displaying was a "co-exist" logo to point to our need for religious tolerance. As more views and ideas become popular, we do need room to discuss, learn, disagree, and respect others. The next generation will need to see that those who worship the

---

1. 1 Pet 3:15.

From Bible as Textbook to Inexhaustible Treasure

Prince of Peace can[2] model a new way of peace in pluralistic times. As we planted a church in a secular community, we dealt with many questions related to other religions and the issues of division among Christians. Armed with historical references, those in a secular age default to minimizing the influence of all religions. This is not helpful, but it is a common reaction. As we deal with this new reality, we must remember that people are still searching for and seeking what is actually true.

We need to understand that diverse religious traditions answer questions of truth, meaning, and significance very differently.[3] As we acknowledge this, we create room for discussions that allow us to understand these differences and to return to the rich theological treasures found in the Bible. When this is not possible, old and naïve caricatures take root that strengthen an unnecessary resistance towards the Bible.

At the same time, I am learning that some of the resistance we see in a secular culture is not necessarily rooted in rejection. It can be more subtle and complex. As I lead and learn from within our context, I have remarked that for many the confusion and frustration related to church, the Bible, and faith in God finds its roots in stories of pain. Soon the importance of the Bible is overshadowed by these struggles, which leads people to conclude that the Bible is an outdated religious textbook for religious types. It is my hope that this chapter will provide some wisdom for how to correct another misconception the distorts the nature of the Bible.

A textbook view of the Bible blinds us from hearing the words of the Bible as a treasure of ever-living truth and wisdom. Alister McGrath, a leading Oxford theologian, observed: "The Church has always struggled to find the right words to describe the treasure that has been entrusted to it—a treasure upon which its identity and survival depends."[4] One step toward finding the right, or new, words, involves correcting the hurdles created by old words and listening for the ways pain and pride often inform how issues in our secular contexts influence beliefs about the Bible.

The urgency for reimagining the Bible as a treasure of living truths comes on the heels of a growing interest in spirituality, which includes a renewed interest in ancient teachings. Just a few days ago, I saw a video interview where famous comedian Jerry Seinfeld, when talking about his career, mentioned the importance of mediation and the Stoic principles of

---

2. Isa 9:6.

3. See Prothero, *God Is Not One*.

4. McGrath, *What's the Point of Theology?*, 130.

Emperor Marcus Aurelius.[5] Closer to home, I remember a discussion with a guest visiting our church. They talked about summer pool parties and without a pause asked me about palm readers and meditation corners. As I inquired, I learned that this event was part of a late-night "manifesting" experience that included inspirational and destiny visions related to business, romance, and the future.[6] I am learning that these types of examples are more common as people are hungry for help. Accordingly, we see a mix of esoteric beliefs, ancient philosophies, and the endless human struggle to link our desires for significance and a meaningful destiny.

Throughout this book, I have described certain secular shifts as a way of understanding our human longing for a life worth living. In the previous chapter I tied it to our need for purpose. In this chapter I want to spend time thinking about the Bible and our need for stable wisdom like a priceless treasure worth searching for. Popular podcaster Tim Ferris is one of many online influencers now teaching "how to apply Stoic philosophy to your life" with online videos.[7] An evolutionary biologist offers a TED talk on a similar theme hitting over two million views.[8] Even *Elle* magazine points to a turn to ancient wisdom for modern living.[9] To this we might even add the uber-famous Jordan Peterson and his reconnection to ancient philosophy with his popular YouTube series *Ancient Wisdom at an Ancient Library*.[10]

While there is no way to predict where these shifts will lead, I remain convinced that these examples reveal a shocking shift at the heart of this secular age. It is one that involves searching for more rooted and often ancient ways to define a meaningful life and the exploration of lost wisdom for navigating turbulent times. As the frantic pace of life, common in our secular age, continues, we may find new opportunities for expressing how the Bible invites us to hear God's loving words as *trusted* wisdom for changing times. When this happens, we can develop an ability to discern between God-honoring wisdom that finds its apex in Jesus and other popular wisdom streams.

Many in this secular age will need help to reconnect with the world of the Bible since it is the only place for true wisdom about who we are,

---

5. See Aurelius, *Meditations*.
6. McGurk, "Making Dreams Come True."
7. Ferris, "How to Apply Stoic Philosophy to Your Life."
8. Pigliucci, "Stoicism as a Philosophy for an Ordinary Life."
9. Bird, "Rise of Modern Stoicism."
10. Peterson, *Ancient Wisdom at an Ancient Library*.

and why Jesus' teachings remain timeless for any age. A hindrance to this is a textbook view of the Bible, which blinds us to the good news of Jesus' ways. My hope is that the insights of this chapter will shift our thinking and our conversations to demonstrate how the Bible is a treasure trove of living wisdom that points to a different kind of centeredness, one which alleviates certain pressures associated with this shifting age.[11]

MODERN PROBLEMS AND THE INVENTION OF TEXTBOOKS

A textbook, in the modern sense, is a book that addresses a specific topic, often in an academic context. We have all enjoyed a good textbook, but this experience may skew how we approach a book like the Bible, relegating it to the status of a religious textbook. Soon, even when people read it, it is to get some information about a religious problem or question. This is a modern challenge. Not only does this distort our view of the Bible, but it limits the ways the Bible is meant to address every area of our life. Anyone who reads the Bible knows how its wisdom overflows to address areas of worship, friendships, and finances, while also drawing us toward treasured sacred mysteries.

The blessings of our modern age inevitably create new challenges that many in the Bible did not face. This modern interpretive lens of the world informs how we think of the biblical world. When this modern lens wins out, the idea of the Bible as a textbook soon sets in, and reading the Bible is seen as optional depending on one's degree of religious interest. This has fostered a mental fragmentation that I have noticed even among Christians who respect and love the Bible. You might remember that a secular age is not just somewhere "out there." In this secular age, the Bible is a kind of religious "textbook" that is okay to be read or hear on a Sunday, from a preacher we like—but not too much more. Almost as in a classroom, the information is presented in a "controlled" setting. Consequentially, the living nature of the words often fail to penetrate the rest of life. While some read the Bible and even embrace its moral wisdom, it rarely shifts their thinking and living. Hence, a compartmentalized mindset develops, where God and the Bible are part of our "church mode"—but for the most part, our life is lived on our terms, and we form our own beliefs and opinions as we go.

---

11. "Peace I leave with you; my peace I give to you. Not as the world gives do I give to you. Let not your hearts be troubled, neither let them be afraid" John 14:16 (ESV).

Left unaddressed, this creates an incorrect approach to the Bible that flows neatly into a secular mindset that is showing new openness toward ancient ideas. Soon we start to believe that we can gain Godly wisdom from the Bible while compartmentalizing life based on personal interest. As with apps on our phone, we group together our favorite types of ideas or interests in a way that they do not overlap. I, just like you, have my work, gaming, entertainment, sports, and spirituality/wellness apps. This feels systematic and efficient to a modern person. Unfortunately, it confuses biblical wisdom for tips or inspirational quotes. As we will soon see, the wisdom offered by the Bible is inspired, which is different than inspirational. To miss this is to fail to hear how biblical wisdom is meant to pierce every area of our lives.

Long before our digital challenges, the 1900s revealed the need to grapple with a shift in education as schools reconsidered how to teach about religions based on a textbook. This again was a shift in learning linked to the modern world we explored in previous chapters. Not only was this unfair to religious traditions that did not approach faith through a Western academic lens, it assumed that faith and the Bible, if worth pursuing, should fit a modern Enlightenment paradigm. The Bible was the textbook of Christians, the Quran the text of Muslims, etc. If you have taken a comparative religion course or watched popular documentaries, you have experienced this approach. The Bible is placed alongside other religious books and soon we find ourselves debating which is more valid, accurate, and relevant with consumer interests in mind.

As I write, a *National Geographic* magazine sits on my desk.[12] It is an issue on the Bible, the Dead Sea scrolls, and other historical insights that presents the Bible as important yet as a religious kind of textbook one explores if interested in old religious stuff. I think of many people who find it easy and uninteresting when a type of textbook approach sets in. Soon, they miss out on the richer truth that is available when we shift our thinking about the Bible. While I am in favor of studying the Bible in academic settings, those who struggle with ideas related to religious pluralism will need help to reimagine how the Bible's content reveals a different kind of wisdom.

The wisdom the Bible offers involves slowing down enough to unearth how its addresses the whole human person—our inner emotions, our longing for healing, and our need to hope, dream, and question suffering. This kind of wisdom touches every aspect of human life by using diverse

---

12. *National Geographic*, "Dead Sea Scrolls."

Prince of Peace can[2] model a new way of peace in pluralistic times. As we planted a church in a secular community, we dealt with many questions related to other religions and the issues of division among Christians. Armed with historical references, those in a secular age default to minimizing the influence of all religions. This is not helpful, but it is a common reaction. As we deal with this new reality, we must remember that people are still searching for and seeking what is actually true.

We need to understand that diverse religious traditions answer questions of truth, meaning, and significance very differently.[3] As we acknowledge this, we create room for discussions that allow us to understand these differences and to return to the rich theological treasures found in the Bible. When this is not possible, old and naïve caricatures take root that strengthen an unnecessary resistance towards the Bible.

At the same time, I am learning that some of the resistance we see in a secular culture is not necessarily rooted in rejection. It can be more subtle and complex. As I lead and learn from within our context, I have remarked that for many the confusion and frustration related to church, the Bible, and faith in God finds its roots in stories of pain. Soon the importance of the Bible is overshadowed by these struggles, which leads people to conclude that the Bible is an outdated religious textbook for religious types. It is my hope that this chapter will provide some wisdom for how to correct another misconception the distorts the nature of the Bible.

A textbook view of the Bible blinds us from hearing the words of the Bible as a treasure of ever-living truth and wisdom. Alister McGrath, a leading Oxford theologian, observed: "The Church has always struggled to find the right words to describe the treasure that has been entrusted to it—a treasure upon which its identity and survival depends."[4] One step toward finding the right, or new, words, involves correcting the hurdles created by old words and listening for the ways pain and pride often inform how issues in our secular contexts influence beliefs about the Bible.

The urgency for reimagining the Bible as a treasure of living truths comes on the heels of a growing interest in spirituality, which includes a renewed interest in ancient teachings. Just a few days ago, I saw a video interview where famous comedian Jerry Seinfeld, when talking about his career, mentioned the importance of mediation and the Stoic principles of

---

2. Isa 9:6.

3. See Prothero, *God Is Not One*.

4. McGrath, *What's the Point of Theology?*, 130.

Emperor Marcus Aurelius.[5] Closer to home, I remember a discussion with a guest visiting our church. They talked about summer pool parties and without a pause asked me about palm readers and meditation corners. As I inquired, I learned that this event was part of a late-night "manifesting" experience that included inspirational and destiny visions related to business, romance, and the future.[6] I am learning that these types of examples are more common as people are hungry for help. Accordingly, we see a mix of esoteric beliefs, ancient philosophies, and the endless human struggle to link our desires for significance and a meaningful destiny.

Throughout this book, I have described certain secular shifts as a way of understanding our human longing for a life worth living. In the previous chapter I tied it to our need for purpose. In this chapter I want to spend time thinking about the Bible and our need for stable wisdom like a priceless treasure worth searching for. Popular podcaster Tim Ferris is one of many online influencers now teaching "how to apply Stoic philosophy to your life" with online videos.[7] An evolutionary biologist offers a TED talk on a similar theme hitting over two million views.[8] Even *Elle* magazine points to a turn to ancient wisdom for modern living.[9] To this we might even add the uber-famous Jordan Peterson and his reconnection to ancient philosophy with his popular YouTube series *Ancient Wisdom at an Ancient Library*.[10]

While there is no way to predict where these shifts will lead, I remain convinced that these examples reveal a shocking shift at the heart of this secular age. It is one that involves searching for more rooted and often ancient ways to define a meaningful life and the exploration of lost wisdom for navigating turbulent times. As the frantic pace of life, common in our secular age, continues, we may find new opportunities for expressing how the Bible invites us to hear God's loving words as *trusted* wisdom for changing times. When this happens, we can develop an ability to discern between God-honoring wisdom that finds its apex in Jesus and other popular wisdom streams.

Many in this secular age will need help to reconnect with the world of the Bible since it is the only place for true wisdom about who we are,

---

5. See Aurelius, *Meditations*.
6. McGurk, "Making Dreams Come True."
7. Ferris, "How to Apply Stoic Philosophy to Your Life."
8. Pigliucci, "Stoicism as a Philosophy for an Ordinary Life."
9. Bird, "Rise of Modern Stoicism."
10. Peterson, *Ancient Wisdom at an Ancient Library*.

From Bible as Textbook to Inexhaustible Treasure

and why Jesus' teachings remain timeless for any age. A hindrance to this is a textbook view of the Bible, which blinds us to the good news of Jesus' ways. My hope is that the insights of this chapter will shift our thinking and our conversations to demonstrate how the Bible is a treasure trove of living wisdom that points to a different kind of centeredness, one which alleviates certain pressures associated with this shifting age.[11]

MODERN PROBLEMS AND THE INVENTION OF TEXTBOOKS

A textbook, in the modern sense, is a book that addresses a specific topic, often in an academic context. We have all enjoyed a good textbook, but this experience may skew how we approach a book like the Bible, relegating it to the status of a religious textbook. Soon, even when people read it, it is to get some information about a religious problem or question. This is a modern challenge. Not only does this distort our view of the Bible, but it limits the ways the Bible is meant to address every area of our life. Anyone who reads the Bible knows how its wisdom overflows to address areas of worship, friendships, and finances, while also drawing us toward treasured sacred mysteries.

The blessings of our modern age inevitably create new challenges that many in the Bible did not face. This modern interpretive lens of the world informs how we think of the biblical world. When this modern lens wins out, the idea of the Bible as a textbook soon sets in, and reading the Bible is seen as optional depending on one's degree of religious interest. This has fostered a mental fragmentation that I have noticed even among Christians who respect and love the Bible. You might remember that a secular age is not just somewhere "out there." In this secular age, the Bible is a kind of religious "textbook" that is okay to be read or hear on a Sunday, from a preacher we like—but not too much more. Almost as in a classroom, the information is presented in a "controlled" setting. Consequentially, the living nature of the words often fail to penetrate the rest of life. While some read the Bible and even embrace its moral wisdom, it rarely shifts their thinking and living. Hence, a compartmentalized mindset develops, where God and the Bible are part of our "church mode"—but for the most part, our life is lived on our terms, and we form our own beliefs and opinions as we go.

---

11. "Peace I leave with you; my peace I give to you. Not as the world gives do I give to you. Let not your hearts be troubled, neither let them be afraid" John 14:16 (ESV).

The Bible for a *Shifting Secular Age*

Left unaddressed, this creates an incorrect approach to the Bible that flows neatly into a secular mindset that is showing new openness toward ancient ideas. Soon we start to believe that we can gain Godly wisdom from the Bible while compartmentalizing life based on personal interest. As with apps on our phone, we group together our favorite types of ideas or interests in a way that they do not overlap. I, just like you, have my work, gaming, entertainment, sports, and spirituality/wellness apps. This feels systematic and efficient to a modern person. Unfortunately, it confuses biblical wisdom for tips or inspirational quotes. As we will soon see, the wisdom offered by the Bible is inspired, which is different than inspirational. To miss this is to fail to hear how biblical wisdom is meant to pierce every area of our lives.

Long before our digital challenges, the 1900s revealed the need to grapple with a shift in education as schools reconsidered how to teach about religions based on a textbook. This again was a shift in learning linked to the modern world we explored in previous chapters. Not only was this unfair to religious traditions that did not approach faith through a Western academic lens, it assumed that faith and the Bible, if worth pursuing, should fit a modern Enlightenment paradigm. The Bible was the textbook of Christians, the Quran the text of Muslims, etc. If you have taken a comparative religion course or watched popular documentaries, you have experienced this approach. The Bible is placed alongside other religious books and soon we find ourselves debating which is more valid, accurate, and relevant with consumer interests in mind.

As I write, a *National Geographic* magazine sits on my desk.[12] It is an issue on the Bible, the Dead Sea scrolls, and other historical insights that presents the Bible as important yet as a religious kind of textbook one explores if interested in old religious stuff. I think of many people who find it easy and uninteresting when a type of textbook approach sets in. Soon, they miss out on the richer truth that is available when we shift our thinking about the Bible. While I am in favor of studying the Bible in academic settings, those who struggle with ideas related to religious pluralism will need help to reimagine how the Bible's content reveals a different kind of wisdom.

The wisdom the Bible offers involves slowing down enough to unearth how its addresses the whole human person—our inner emotions, our longing for healing, and our need to hope, dream, and question suffering. This kind of wisdom touches every aspect of human life by using diverse

---

12. *National Geographic,* "Dead Sea Scrolls."

From Bible as Textbook to Inexhaustible Treasure

methods. From historical stories, to parables, to commands and warnings, the Bible comes at our need for wisdom in diverse ways. To clarify, the whole Bible offers us wisdom, yet scholars have also noted a particular category of biblical books that we refer to as wisdom literature.[13]

These books involve short sayings, almost like tweets, that have been passed on as riddles with rich lessons that the wise embrace and the foolish ignore. To help us not ignore them, the wisdom of the Bible is best heard in communal worship, where accountability to others who are also seeking wisdom is made evident. Further, it is in this context that we hear God's loving instruction meant for transformation that extends far beyond our modern problems. I think of ancient prayers wrapped in enduring wisdom that reveal a God who says, "I will give you the treasures of darkness . . . riches hidden in secret places, so that you may know that I am the LORD, the God of Israel, who calls you by name." No textbook can grapple with this kind of wisdom.[14]

When a modern perspective dominates how we approach the Bible, we miss the stream of wisdom and default to a textbook mindset. For some, there also emerges an overreaction to try to defend and prove the Bible's effectiveness in the face of questions. This approach to apologetics loses its biblical roots when it is overshadowed by a modern outlook that, in a subtle way, assumes the Bible is a textbook. We then feel like we must *prove* the authority of the Bible as a religious text. Often, this is done by contrasting and comparing it with other religious books to demonstrate which textbook is really from God. There is a whole industry of debating and defending the Bible like this—and many in a secular age have started to ignore it. It may help us to consider why Jesus rarely engaged in debates the way we do in a modern context. I want to suggest that the wisdom the Bible offers is not internalized through debates. The wisdom of the Bible reveals a treasure that is linked to the *living* truth associated with the *living* Jesus that stirs the mind and the heart of those living it out. Apologetics shaped by more precise information alone miss the essential ways biblical truth and wisdom are offered to us in the Bible. Jesus' wisdom does not fit neatly into a modern view of knowledge. It reminds me of the saying, "A bird sitting on a tree is not afraid of the branch breaking, because her trust is not in the branch but in her wings." A modern textbook approach to the Bible confused the branch for the wings. With Jesus, we are invited to trust

---

13. This includes the Proverbs and book of Ecclesiastes.
14. Isa 45:3.

God because the Bible reveals that only the living Jesus has been given all authority in heaven and on earth.[15]

As debates about the Bible continue, we must pay attention to how a strict textbook lens of the Bible confuses knowledge with wisdom. One way to know that difference is to remember that knowledge is about what we know, and wisdom is about knowing how to apply that knowledge. Both matter, but they are not necessarily the same. Another way to think about it is that biblical wisdom calls us to love what is right, not just to do what is right. Here wisdom makes all the difference. This often confuses those in a secular age. As I speak with those disoriented by a secular age, I find that for them, knowledge and wisdom collapse into a huge blur. This is rooted in a contested view of truth because we struggle to know who we can trust. In those conversations I soon find myself discussing whether we can trust the four differing biographies (Gospels) about Jesus. Few realize it was God-inspired wisdom to provide four perspectives, and not just one, about the life and ministry of Jesus. In fact, I emphasize that it was intentional, and God-ordained, to provide us with four diverse and different perspectives about the life and ministry of Jesus. Comparing or dissecting them as we would an academic textbook only devalues their uniqueness and misses out on the wisdom because of our fascination with a certain view of knowledge.

Once again, the great North African bishop St. Augustine wisely remarked: "The Bible was composed in such a way that as beginners mature, its meaning grows with them."[16] As one grows, God's wisdom increases our capacity to embrace the deeper truths of the Bible. This is not the case with a textbook. Textbooks are important for recording information, but they are not linked to the human longing for ongoing wisdom and guidance that leads to transformation and spiritual maturity. It is paramount that those in a secular age learn to rediscover that the Bible is so much more than a religious textbook.

By now, you have probably sensed the numerous ways our modern world fused with secular values creates new hurdles. I hope you can see how these approaches converge in fostering a detached view of learning. By doing this, the communal essence at the heart of the whole Bible is overlooked, and soon a distorted view that turns the Bible into a religious textbook takes root. Recently, my son missed a class at school. As we chatted, I did the dad thing. I asked if he followed up with the teacher and got

---

15. Matt 28.
16. Augustine, *Confessions*, 3:9.

From Bible as Textbook to Inexhaustible Treasure

the notes for the class from a classmate. As we talked, he said: "Dad, I'm good, I have the textbook." This, for those in our present context, becomes the default for private, self-serving, and random interactions with the Bible. It is the naive belief that if you have the textbook (your own Bible) you'll be fine. This faulty outlook minimizes the importance of trusted voices like teachers, and one's interactive presence linked to a Christian understanding of accountability, living with and among others.

For the rest of this chapter, I want to revisit a biblical image to reconnect the Bible as living words to the image of a treasure. Jesus, when teaching, used words like "seeking" and "searching" when speaking about the essence of his mission. This is *discovering treasure* language, and it is meant to evoke the ongoing discovery of wisdom available for those who trust in God's ways. In addition, the God we meet in the pages of the Bible speaks of his creation, in particular us humans, as a lost treasure being recovered and restored to its rightful place. To hear and embrace this truth, we must put the Bible in its rightful place so that the living words are heard correctly and obeyed as God's wisdom for us today.

LESSONS FROM CLEANING OFF A BURIED TREASURE

The image of a treasure is one that resonates in numerous cultures, and it is an ancient image used in the Bible. Thinking of the wisdom God has for us, the Bible, speaking of God's insights, states, "Search for them as you would for silver; seek them like hidden treasures. Then you will understand what it means to fear the Lord, and you will gain knowledge of God."[17] This Old Testament invitation points to our need. Further, in the New Testament we also read of transformative encounters involving the discovery of God's words as living words. Acts 17 explores how wisdom and cultural engagement became one method Paul used when addressing the issues of his changing culture. This intense encounter involves Paul's address to the philosophical elites of Athens. I encourage you to read it in its entirety.

When you read it, notice that the context has some resemblance to key issue we have noted in our secular age. Not only did Paul address numerous religious spiritual options, but he was also aware of the suspicion a new religion like Christianity caused in the surrounding pluralistic culture. In this context, Paul is seen as a foreigner bringing new ideas that are very

---

17. Prov 2:4–5 (NLT).

confusing. Moreover, we are provided with biblical wisdom that reminds us that there was a time when Christianity was the new faith tradition on the block. Although it resembled and grew out of Judaism, it was heard as a new kind of wisdom.

As Paul engages with those who did not understand how the resurrection could be good news for humanity, we read:

> Because Paul was preaching the good news about Jesus and the resurrection ... they took him and brought him to a meeting of the Areopagus, where they said to him, "May we know what this new teaching is that you are presenting? You are bringing some strange ideas to our ears, and we would like to know what they mean."[18]

The first century, in some ways, points to similar themes apparent in our secular age. Not only was the message of Christianity new, but the rich truths that were being offered were not easily understood. The treasured wisdom of it all could only be discovered as people asked questions and *uncovered* its deeper meaning. This continues to be true as we help people read and engage with the Bible in new ways. We must be okay with questions as well as moments of frustration from inquirers. Further, this process of exploring the Christian faith and biblical wisdom for the life we are meant to live is made possible because of Jesus' resurrection. For that reason Paul makes it the heart of the Christian wisdom tradition.

Just as one might unearth a treasure covered with dirt, brushing it off and turning it to see its many facets, so we need to help inquirers investigate the Bible as unexpected treasure. It is a treasure covered by modern assumptions, painful stories of betrayal, the habit of compartmentalization, and a blind spot in seeing the Bible as a textbook. When we dig up and dust off the Bible, embracing it as a unique treasure, we begin to hear the deep, God-inspired wisdom that takes us beyond mere knowledge and information. I have seen firsthand how people experience their eyes and ears opening as the Bible's wisdom speaks into their situation. With that comes a fresh passion to believe that what we have in the Bible is a priceless treasure still reflecting the goodness of God to us. Further, it should lead to a desire to read it more consistently.

As we clean off the layers of dirt we adjust our gaze. As we do this, we are wise to remember that from the earliest days of the Christianity the Bible and the deeper truth it points to were heard as "strange ideas."

---

18. Acts 17:18–20.

From Bible as Textbook to Inexhaustible Treasure

The good news is that we are not the first to learn how to clarify God's wisdom for shifting times. One step forward is to know our context, to humbly acknowledge that it's normal to be confused, and to encourage ongoing questions about what is true and trustworthy. In God's mysterious timing, we listen for ways to help others embrace the treasured things God is revealing. In addition, this rooted biblical approach avoids the common secular temptation to engage in unnecessary confrontation.

The Areopagus, which Paul eventually got an audience with, was the official council of those who monitored new religious teachers in the area. Paul likely knew that meeting with them and explaining the good news was a strategic step for expressing the wisdom of Jesus in a world of spiritual options. Like getting an interview with the CEO as part of a hiring process, or a chance to make a pitch on *Shark Tank*, this would have felt like a God moment. I reminded of how it felt when city officials inquired about our church plant. Understandably, they were unsure about a new church meeting in a warehouse space. It was the wisdom in this biblical passage that guided us as we welcomed the conversation and heard their valid concerns and questions. While it was not all pleasant, I can attest that God's wisdom prevailed, as there was an openness and respect that led to a permanent space for our church to meet. From this small yet significant experience, we were learning to apply God's biblical wisdom as we modeled that we also care about the community and many issues impacting all of us struggling through the shifts of a secular age.

A last image that comes to mind is that of clearing the dirt off the treasure of the Bible; this image helps others embrace its reliability and durability as a book that has withstood significant critique. This should alleviate a common attitude of Christians who feel unease about the secular world posing questions about our faith. Again, if the Bible is just a religious textbook that we put up against other religious texts, we feel threatened by the questions posed by a "bad" world. I recently struggled with this inner tension as I listened to a popular entertainer use the Bible as a prop, a type of textbook, for his comedy act.

The clip I saw was from comedian Louis C. K., who, as part of his show, started reading the Bible live during his act.[19] Yes, in the secular age of 2023. A sold-out crowd heard him comment on Jesus' cursing a fig tree. Between numerous expletives and comical reading from the King James version, he emphasized how "cranky Jesus" curses a fig tree. To the laughter-filled room

---

19. Louis C. K., *Back to the Garden*.

he pointed out the strangeness of the story. He's got a point, but only if one never learns that the Bible is meant to be read and heard as a rich treasure of stories that have a deeper meaning that are easily missed at first glance. The wisdom of the fig tree story, at least in Mark's Gospel, is linked to the cleansing of the temple. To disconnect the stories is to miss the larger point filled with relevant wisdom related to injustice that those in secular age would appreciate deeply.

While some may be offended at these kinds of at the jabs towards the Christians and Jews, I paused to prayerfully consider if maybe these habits of non-Christian readings of the Bible may be linked to the strange methods they learned from Christians. I have seen how Christians pick and choose random stories and use them to fit their own narrative. Some, informed by an anti-intellectual mindset, ignore the importance of theological reflection and thoughtful insights by well-respected scholars. Can we then really be shocked when those in a secular culture read the Bible in ways that lack wisdom?

It has never been more important to recommit to the hard work that leads others to hear the Bible as wisdom we discover, the kind of wisdom that may be tested and that anchors us in a larger story. This story overflows with wisdom to awaken us to God's loving ways and his redemptive plans. One reason that jokes about the Bible land well in this secular age is that people assume that its stories were from ancient times that do not any longer apply to us. Because of this, many are convinced that these laughs and jokes are not intended to be disrespectful. While you and I may disagree, we are wise to understand where they might be coming from. It is for this reason that we must model what it means to hear and present the Bible as living truth, from a living God, as we correct and address misguided beliefs.

A TREASURE THAT INCREASES IN VALUE

One day an older woman visiting our church waited until after our morning gathering to chat. There was a sheepish way about her. Soon she mustered the courage to ask, "Where does the Bible talk about dating later in life?" Being in her mid-fifties and wondering about how to move on after a painful relationship, she was seeking wisdom. As you might agree, moments like this require pastoral sensitivity as we listen and do our best to care. I could sense her unspoken loneliness and longing for companionship as we spoke. However, I was also aware that the Bible was vastly different, especially as it related to dating later in life. Questions about dating, parenting, technology, and other complex global concerns are not just a Bible verse away. For this, we need to reimagine the Bible as living wisdom, not just static knowledge.

In my response to her question, I suggested a fuller picture of the Bible, much as I am doing in this book. I said: "Imagine that the Bible does not address our deepest longing in a clean, encyclopedic, or textbook-like way. Instead, it is a 'book' filled with stories rooted in truth and wisdom that we must explore and discover as we search and discern what God is saying to us today." Her eyes lit up as she said, "Wow, that's what the Bible is?" It was one of those moments where I realized how important a "treasure" image of the Bible will be for those who are living in the complexities of unforeseen life issues while realizing that this world has not delivered in addressing our deepest human questions about life, meaning, and truth.

The Bible as a treasure allows us to reinforce the gift of *ongoing* wisdom, which is more valuable than we often imagine. The American poet Robinson Jeffers wrote: "Stars burn, grass grows, men breathe: as a man finding treasure says 'Ah!' but the treasure's the essence; Before the man spoke it was there, and after he has spoken he gathers it, inexhaustible treasure."[20] I love the image of a treasure as ever present, and that outlasts our fleeting concerns. This profound image of awareness that speaks to the timelessness and inexhaustible issues we associate with words like *awe, mystery, destiny*, all found in the rich pages of the Bible. When we keep reading the Bible, its truth sets in as inexhaustible, even if at first glance we do not notice. This is the nature of this God-inspired treasure, meant to keep guiding us to discover the life we were meant to live.

A secular age awash in a tsunami of quick-fix tips and life hacks will continue to show signs of weariness linked to fleeting attempts for stability. The wisdom found in the Bible is God's gift to instruct us in discernment, discipleship, and spiritual maturity, an anchor for shifting times, not just answers. Some have proposed the treasure image by thinking of a precious diamond. As the light reflects on a diamond it shines as new and unexpected colors are revealed and light and beauty conjure up more appreciation for the kind of gem that it is.

The Bible, because it alone is inspired by the Holy Spirit, is similar. The light of the Spirit shines and draws out reliable wisdom that we keep coming back to even today. One example can be seen in Paul's wisdom

---

20. Jeffers, "Treasure," lines 12–15.

about the theme of love. Over the past few weeks, I have met with diverse people, many fully engaged in a secular way of life yet wondering about love beyond fleeting feelings. I have often asked if they are familiar with the famous Bible passage on love. It goes like this:

> Love is patient, love is kind. It does not envy, it does not boast, it is not proud. It does not dishonor others, it is not self-seeking, it is not easily angered, it keeps no record of wrongs. Love does not delight in evil but rejoices with the truth. It always protects, always trusts, always hopes, always perseveres. Love never fails. But where there are prophecies, they will cease; where there are tongues, they will be stilled; where there is knowledge, it will pass away.[21]

My inquirers are not shocked when they hear this, since they remember it from a marriage celebration. Intentionally I remind them these words about love were firstly a grounding vision of love, filled with wisdom and truth, for those learning to love one another as a struggling church working through painful disunity. Most are shocked but then soon inquire to learn more. After this *initial* truth about this passage takes root we seek to understand even more wisdom. Just like multifaceted light reflecting on a diamond, we move to the extended secondary wisdom available. What if now, this image of love helps us consider the dangers of disunity in marriage?

With that first and essential lens of interpretation we now add a new application. The Bible, a living treasure, is still speaking to a modern culture that approaches marriage very differently than those in the Bible. All of us need constant reformation of our views about love. Paul was inspired by the Holy Spirit to address particular situations, yet we must return to the Bible to be heard as God's living word of a love that will heal our deepest propensity for division. It is no surprise that Paul, in his Letter to the Ephesians, offers a different, yet similar picture of a church associated with the love of a bride and groom.[22] For this reason, it can be just as beautiful to also hear these verses at a wedding. Every generation will have to learn to read and hear the Bible in a proper way that provides a *reliable* interpretation rooted in living wisdom. This is the gift of the Bible that continues to offer fresh treasured wisdom. When this is lost, we experience what I call a hermeneutic of detachment.

---

21. 1 Cor 13:4–8 (NIV).
22. Eph 5.

From Bible as Textbook to Inexhaustible Treasure

ATTITUDES FOR SPOTTING WISDOM

Hermeneutics is a theological word that involves the *skillful* art of interpretation. When used for the Bible it involves a deep awareness of the way we are prone to interpret or misinterpret the Bible. One of my professors used to say, "You can only learn what the Bible is *for* you when you remember it was *not* written *to* you." This insight requires interpretive awareness that many miss in the accelerated and detached ways of learning of our secular age. A detached interpretation bypasses the patience from which wisdom emerges. It assumes answers are fast and ideas must point to pragmatic ends. For some, this means we should just bring our problems, questions, and experiences to the Bible and find the answers we want when we want them. Again, it's a textbook ideology.

However, the Bible itself calls us to "let your roots grow down into him, and let your lives be built on him. Then your faith will grow strong in the truth you were taught."[23] This is wisdom-based root system, familiar to those in the Bible, and always interconnected with other Christians seeking God's wisdom as well. In the living community of the church, we must push back against the detached textbook perspectives. Here the living wisdom of the Bible clarifies and corrects how to respond—we listen and learn with others.

The Bible as a treasure provides new words, which includes a new perspective to talk about what is most important about the living truth of Jesus. In English the word *thesaurus* comes from the Greek word for treasure. Some of you might already see the link. If you have used a thesaurus, you know it is a book that gives options of words to reimagine and give fresh perspective for a word that may have lost its intended meaning. Those in a secular culture wondering about meaning may need to be led to hear a "thesaurus"-shaped understanding of the Bible, one that points to a God who has more wisdom than we will ever need.

Jesus knew what it was like for a word to lose its meaning. One word that had lost its ability to grip people was the word *neighbor*. This is a treasured word that Jesus invited his first listeners, and now us, to reimagine. He did this by adding new value and a richer interpretation that involves new wisdom and a surrender of old categories. Luke recounts the story of an expert in the Torah, the leading teacher of the Jewish people, who came with a question/test for Jesus. "'Teacher,' he asked, 'what must I do to

---

23. Col 2:6–7 (NLT).

inherit eternal life?' 'What is written in the Law?' he replied. 'How do you read it?'"[24]

How do you read it? This is a question linked to hermeneutics. Jesus instructs this teacher by calling his attention to the layers of meaning that reveal deeper treasures of wisdom. In a similar way Jesus is still doing this with us as we consider the secular shifts in our day. In the process, we must get honest about how we misread the Bible as well. It is important to note that this religious leader knew that Jesus was offering a new way to hear and understand the Torah, one that was likely uncomfortable and required change. Jesus flipped the script and then he was the one offering a test—not a trick, since Jesus was not vindictive.

Soon, the discussion moves to the meaning of the word *neighbor*. Just like today the word *neighbor* had fallen on a slippery slope of meaninglessness. Jesus, aware of that, does not offer a definition but instead tells a story. It's a moment to savor the rich, wise ways for learning that crushes the efficiency models we are accustomed to. Stories take time to develop and time to interpret. Known as one of the great Bible stories even by those outside of the Christian tradition, Jesus' parable is known as the Good Samaritan. It could have been easily called the Stubborn and Silly Torah Teacher, but the shocking fact that a Samaritan would teach a Jew—who was a Torah expert—would not have been missed by the earliest listeners. If you can, pause and read the whole story for yourself.[25] What living wisdom stands out? Jesus reattached his wisdom to how we care about those around us. This does so much more than clarify that right definition for the word *neighbor*. A textbook would do for that.

As we move from the textbook approach to a treasured engagement with the Bible, we get closer to a hermeneutical lens that corrects a detached reading people are used to. This involves two key attitudes: our posture and our position. By posture, I mean that all encounters with the Bible should foster a posture of humility. Textbooks provide knowledge. The more knowledge we get the less humble we tend to be. The Bible provides a different approach to knowledge rooted in wisdom to remind us that God is at work in ways we will never fully understand on this side of heaven. Here, the limitation of our humanity slaps us in the face, because no matter how "enlightened" we may be, that is not to be equated with the

---

24. Luke 10:25–26.
25. Found in Luke 10:29–37.

treasured wisdom of the Bible. More wisdom always fosters more humility, which draws us back to our limited understanding.

A humble posture adjusts our interpretive lens to notice our limits. This truth is rooted in biblical wisdom all the way to the first chapters of the Bible. Again, just as with fresh light on a diamond we see something new. One aspect of our limitation is that we have a limited perspective no matter how knowledgeable we become. This helps us rediscover that while our present context matters, it is not the only perspective, maybe not even the wisest perspective. Humility and limitation recall for us that for thousands of years other Christians, in different cultures, from different ethnic backgrounds, from diverse linguistic and socioeconomic contexts have sought wisdom from the same heard and read words, from the same Bible we read today. Humility awakens our need to acknowledge that we are attached to a long legacy of wisdom seekers whenever we read the Bible. I regularly remind our church: "Christianity did not begin when you became a Christian." This is important for engaging a secular age that is sensitive to reaffirm the nature of local communities in the face of oppressive universal narratives that have used power to silence diversity.

A posture of humility corrects a modern arrogance about the ancient world. Jesus spoke and taught among many who were illiterate. Yes, not only could they not read, but they were also not in a hurry to learn how to read. Their world was an oral culture in which learning involved memorization, repeated storytelling, and lots of singing, all done in community. Reading was likely linked to the rabbinic schools and synagogues, yet the average person had ears attuned to picking up key stories. In an oral, agrarian culture education functioned differently. Systematized knowledge, as we expect with a textbook, was not a priority for hearing and responding to the good news. This in no way is meant to minimize the need for our methods of learning, but is meant to keep things in context. Consider that the New Testament does not even present the books we have in chronological order and chapter and verse numbers are likely a fourteenth-century addition.[26] All this points to the Bible as living words of wisdom that are still revealing truth we need, but not in the ways we would expect.

---

26. The first Gospel was Mark, and the earliest book of the New Testament was likely the letter we call 1 Thessalonians or the Letter to the Galatians.

THE BIBLE FOR A *SHIFTING* SECULAR AGE

THE TREASURY: LESSONS FROM OUR AFRICAN BROTHER

My heart for the global church and its interpretive wisdom keeps expanding. I hope you feel the same way. This is an important moment of realization for Western Christians, recognizing that future leaders for engaging with our secular culture will likely come from the developing world. Those first followers of Jesus were holding on to a treasure, a spiritual *AllSpark* for you *Transformer* movie fans, that had creative capacity beyond their imagination. The book of Acts describes some of the fast-moving, shocking, revealing, and messy "global" interactions ancient wisdom and new knowledge seem to create when they collide.

In Acts 8 we read of an important dignitary in charge of the treasures of a queen. As an esteemed leader he is described as one who, in addition to having wealth and influence, sought out something more. He reminds us of our own need to have a life built on that which is not fleeting. This man from Ethiopia brings us face to face with the hyper-pluralism of the first century: the options were endless.

When we are introduced to him, this unnamed man, who is also described as a eunuch, is reading from the Jewish Scriptures. Yes, a non-Jew, reading from a book equated with the ancient wisdom of the Jewish people. This might sound strange, but just like today, it was seen as positive to mix beliefs and even worship diverse gods in hopes of gaining their favor. Think back to the God-fearers we discussed earlier. As we continue reading in Acts 8, our attention is turned to Philip, an early follower of Jesus. Following a local persecution, Philip is prompted by God to attend to the questions of this searching Ethiopian. It's almost like God wants to remind us that seasons of persecution are no match for the treasured ways he will continue to reveal his love.

Because the Bible is not a textbook meant to just be read privately, we learn that it is the work of the Holy Spirit who clarifies and meets us in our questions. This is exactly what the Ethiopian will need. The same Holy Spirit who inspired the words of the Bible now awakens Philip to participate in providing clarity for this Ethiopian. This begins in a vision when Philip is told: "Go south to the road—the desert road—that goes down from Jerusalem to Gaza." He is not given that reason or the next steps. But the Bible says, "So he started out."[27]

---

27. Acts 8:26–27.

From Bible as Textbook to Inexhaustible Treasure

The desert roads he would have traveled were not safe. Strange travelers as well as unexpected animals along the sixty-two-mile stretch made this trip one that most would avoid. Yet, convinced God was speaking, Philip goes. Then things get even more interesting. We read:

> On his way he met an Ethiopian eunuch, an important official in charge of all the treasury of the *Kandake* (which means "queen of the Ethiopians"). This man had gone to Jerusalem to worship, and on his way home was sitting in his chariot reading the Book of Isaiah the prophet.[28]

Here a non-Jew, from a foreign land, is reading one of the major prophets of Israel. Just like today people who pick up the Bible and read it may experience a similar reality, a mixture of interest and longing wrapped up in confusion. The fact that this notable leader has a copy of Isaiah alerts us to his esteemed position. However, having a book of the Bible or even reading it does not mean one can fully appreciate the wisdom it offers.

I have been blessed to visit and teach in Ethiopia. I have seen firsthand the rich and diverse cultural expressions of Christians bubbling up among a people who have suffered much and who continue to seek God for their families and their land. The story of Christianity is still unfolding in this beautiful part of the world, and it most likely got its start with Philip's obedience to respond to a seeking traveler still reimagining the life he was meant to live. While we know that the Ethiopian eunuch did not need to be told to read the Bible, he did need help to make sense of what he was reading.

Philip's obedience and the eunuch's honesty create a convergence moment. We read: "The Spirit told Philip, 'Go to that chariot and stay near it.' Then Philip ran up to the chariot and heard the man reading Isaiah the prophet. 'Do you understand what you are reading?' Philip asked."[29] In biblical times, people, if they could read, read out loud. Our modern practice of silent reading was not customary. Hence, this practice made it easier for Philip, from memory, to hear and link what was being read to the words of Isaiah and the questions of the eunuch.

I think it fair to say that the Holy Spirit who had led him now prompts him to inquire further, revealing what I believe is one of most crucial questions of our time: "Do you understand what you are reading?" It links us

---

28. Acts 8:26–28.
29. Acts 8:29–30.

back to Jesus' question: "How do you read this?"[30] It's an invitation to have a dialogue and to consider that here is more wisdom than one might first notice. The Bible's salvific treasures are not unearthed alone. Philip's question remains a starting point still today, as we navigate the shifts of our secular age and offer a paradigm shift about the Bible.

"Do you understand?" creates room to admit when we did not understand. This can create safe spaces that minimize shame around learning the Bible. Consider that Philip did not say things that many say from the pulpit that those in our secular age associate with guilt, pressure, and intimidation, like: "Oh finally you are getting into the word of God." Instead, he comes near to ask: "Do you understand what you are reading?" The Ethiopian answers and says: "How can I [understand] unless someone explains it to me?" So, he invites Philip to enter the chariot and sit with him.[31]

WHO IS REALLY DOING THE SEARCHING?

The rest of the story provides a beautiful unveiling of how God's love works in mysterious ways. If you read the story in its entirety, and I hope you do, Philip's explanation of Isaiah causes the eunuch to be baptized. Philip explains, somehow, that Isaiah was foretelling of a time when faithful obedience to Jesus would require a command he left with his followers: Be baptized. How Philip gets from Isaiah to the importance of baptism is an unrevealed mystery. I guess some treasures are meant to remain hidden, but we can imagine it involved gentle questions and lots of listening.

I started this chapter with the complex ways a textbook approach to the Bible pushes us further and further away from an image that can penetrate the nuanced resistance of a secular age. This comes at a time when, just like in the early church, curiosity and links to ancient wisdom are more evident as old narratives are being stretched. It is unimaginable that we would ignore our duty to attend to a shifting secular culture that will wonder why the Bible remains essential to hear and know the living ways of Jesus. Perhaps you never saw your story, your context as a place to share about the rich, treasured truths meant to opened up for others. I hope I can encourage you to see that it has never been more important to affirm, as did

---

30. Luke 10:26.
31. Acts 8:31.

Augustine, that we should all grow in our desire "to see the treasure of the Lord distributed."[32]

When my kids were younger, we lived near a beach. Frequently, we found ourselves digging up rocks and shells. They would get so excited. I can still hear them running over to ask: "Dad, is this a treasure?" I would jokingly respond: "Maybe it's a dinosaur bone or a special rock." They would pause in awe and run off and keep looking for more. Similarly, there is something special and childlike when we believe that we have discovered something rare, valuable, and priceless in the pages of the living words of the Bible. The only response is to keep coming and going back for more.

The corrective shift I have described is meant to alter our thinking, and that of others. As we move from a textbook approach to something more biblical, we become more confident to engage with those in secular age. Moreover, we may be shocked to find how open they are to the unique wisdom found in the living words of Scripture. Jesus' invitation to "Seek first the Kingdom of God and all his right and holy ways"[33] points to the fact that we are all created to seek, to search, even as we struggle to find true wisdom to build our lives on. Those in a secular age want this as well, and they might just be ready to see that one of the greatest treasures revealed to us in the Bible is that God is also seeking after us, his most precious treasure.

---

32. Augustine, "On the Catechizing of the Uninstructed," 1:2.
33. Matt 6:33.

CHAPTER 6

From the Bible as a Rule Book to the Bible as a Guide for Restored Relationships

"Christianity thus tells a true story about humanity that makes sense of all the stories that humanity tells about itself." [1] –Alister McGrath

THE BIBLE AND OUR AI FUTURE

YUVAL HARARI, A HISTORIAN/FUTURIST, recently suggested that tech advances in Artificial Intelligence may lead to a new religion. According to him, this may include a new kind of "Bible" written entirely by a nonhuman entity. In one interview he remarked: "Think of holy books written by AI. That could be a reality in a few years."[2] Harari's comments caused a stir, but for the wrong reasons. While many heard these comments as a warning of a tech world out of control, few picked up on his misunderstanding about what holy books, like the Bible, are actually about.

For Harari, holy books are mostly old myths about humanity's projection of the divine. Hence, it makes sense that we would just make up new religious books as *our* ideas about the divine dissipate and change. As old religious books lose their ability to speak with precision about future realities, why not let AI provide a new way? Unfortunately, this view of the Bible is both common and embraced by many in a secular culture. As we have already seen, our culture and the values of a secular age inform us in subtle ways. The impact of this is that we lose our perspective and diverse

---

1. McGrath, *Narrative Apologetics*, 46.
2. Harari and Pinto, "Humanity Is Not That Simple."

anxieties set in as we think about the changes of the future. Soon we forget that the Bible has, for thousands of years, withstood other eras of immense change.

We have been mapping ways to address misguided views about the Bible while also recognizing the changes emerging from a shifting secular age. No doubt new levels of complexity await. Nevertheless, these debates about the future should push us to consider the questions related to what will makes the future worth living. It's this truth that the Bible addresses. Although Harari's vision of holy books might provide *more accurate* information about future problems, they will not be enough to make life worth living. For this we need to reclaim the way the Bible addresses both changing realities and our human need for living words of truth, anchored in eternal wisdom for flourishing relationships.

The more things change the more intentional we must be to revisit why a secular culture continues to display deep fragmentation in our relationships. Both families and friendships are essential for whatever the future holds. And rules, no matter how accurate, will not address the deep dynamic of healthy relationships. Recently, I used ChatGPT to get advice for a pastoral crisis. ChatGPT is one of many AI tools that will likely revolutionize learning and information sharing. Partly due to curiosity, I asked ChatGPT: "What is the best way to help someone dying of cancer?" Almost instantaneously I got a list of helpful steps, which concluded by suggesting I find a *human* person to talk with. It was good news to see our smartest tech recognize its limits. Maybe it is smarter than we thought.

Clearly, we are living at a time when ethical issues related to AI will need our attention. Further, these issues will cause us to reconsider how we define a moral life that is part of our shared humanity. But the vision to grapple with these issues rests on our ability to embrace the essentials as they relate to the fragmented state of our relationships. This chapter, like the others, is rooted in a biblical vision of bridge-building that extends out to address the broken realities of secular culture. While we have redefined "secular" as open and curious, it will also likely not reciprocate the offer to always cooperate with all things Christian. Yet the Bible commands those who follow it to extend a hand and be Christlike as we notice the signs of people treading water while they deal with relational fragmentation.

Since those in secular age will need practical handles for re-engaging with the Bible, I have tried to provide images that are linked to themes like purpose and wisdom. In this chapter I want us to consider how a new image of the Bible points to much needed hope in the face of numerous struggles that make giving up relationships common. It might come as a shock, but we actually have a whole new vocabulary for how we express the present state of relational disorientation. Terms like *ghosting* and *breadcrumbing* are some of my most popular ones I have heard.[3]

As we present the Bible as living words for restoring our relationships, I think we must develop an inner strength to listen to the painful issues that cause lasting conflict in relationships. Issues like betrayal, death, revenge, and unforgiveness are just a few that crush our human sense of hope and our desire to keep working toward healthy relationships. The good news is that the Bible has much to say about these kinds of issues. Sadly, though, many have assumed that the Bible is an outdated book of rules with little to offer in the face of despair. Subsequently, the hope that it provides remains beyond reach. What is needed is a fresh lens that helps people return to the Bible and embrace how it addresses our spiritual questions, which are often, if not always, intertwined with relational ones.

Maybe you know someone who has a rule-based view of the Bible. My earliest assumption about the Bible was that the whole Bible was a long list of rules, a list of rules that came from some mountain via an old guy with a long beard. Similar to the Ten Commandments, I assumed that the rest of the Bible was made up of thousands of rules or commands with some old stories mixed in. That lens of the Bible as a rule book turned me into a young Christian who believed following Jesus was about following rules. The larger hope-filled experiences of being loved and the joy of engaging with others was not at all possible with this mindset.

I soon learned that a "rule follower" uses the Bible to measure things. I wondered if I measured up to others. Soon I put pressure on others to follow the rules as well. When they did not follow the rules, I became judgmental. I wish someone would have helped me to move beyond this approach by showing me that flourishing human relationships need more than rules and that the Bible, when read properly, addresses that. For that reason, this chapter will consider how to explore the Bible as a book of hope-filled stories that address our need for rooted and restored relationships. This longing is an overflow of being created in the image of a God whose very essence is relational: a Trinitarian being.

Although the Bible does have sections or passage with rules, they are always meant to be heard as loving prayers, proverbs, and promises for

---

3. *Fast Company*, "Ghosted, Orbited, Breadcrumbed."

The Bible as Guide for Restored Relationships

restored relationships. Many in our secular age miss the deep relational nuances that the biblical context assumes. For many people with little or no knowledge of the biblical world, it's easy to defer to everything in the Bible as rules. In fact, in our culture rules are associated with things like sports, where a referee monitors our every move. Rules set boundary markers to know who wins and who loses. Conversely, the biblical narrative is meant to be understood as an expanding story of love, betrayal, rescue, and redemption, offering hope to those who are lost and who can still be found: this is relationship language.

A DISTORTED VIEW: THE BIBLE AS A RULE BOOK

When seeing the Bible as a rule book is not addressed, we even hear God's loving instruction as rules delivered with a divinely ordained hammer. This only stirs suspicion in those shaped by a secular age, who are haunted by stories of religious abuse. Recently, a couple asked to meet with me. They were newer to the church and were nervous about next steps of commitment due to a painful experience at a previous church. At its core, their concern involved pressure they felt to give thousands of dollars for fear of disobeying the rules that the pastor said were in the Bible. As we spoke, I realized how much is at stake if we do not correct this rules-based view of the Bible. Although that local church is now gone, I am ever aware that even after a church is shut down, we cannot underestimate the scars it leaves if the Bible is presented as a rule book. While generosity is a biblical principle, if devoid from the larger love story of a God who cares about us, even good instruction is misunderstood and misapplied.

A rule-book approach to the Bible makes it unimaginable that the words found in it are living words from a living God. From economic concerns to global injustice, those in a secular age are not immune to silent anxieties that cause them to wonder if there is a God who really cares for us. Moreover, the Bible as a rule book only fuels the image of a distant God, a cranky grandpa in the sky, detached from common relational discouragement that eventually finds us all. Many in our culture are working out the pain of broken relationships, fractured marriages, and a divided world all in isolation, unaware of the hope and courage the Bible offers. At its worst, some soon believe that God only shows up when we break the rules. Kind of like the Lorax.

The good news is that our secular age has not silenced our deep desire for trusted relational connection with God and with others. In her masterful book *When God Talks Back*, Tanya Luhrmann describes different ways people continue to explore this human longing for relational connection with the divine. While her findings lead to more questions than answers, the stories point to an undeniable truth: we want to believe that there is a way to have a real relational connection with a God who cares about our lives.

The Bible points to this universal hunger in our shared humanity to know and to be known in a relational way. If you read Acts 17, as I suggested in the previous chapter, you probably remember Paul speaking to those in the city of Athens. In part of his speech, he points to the fact that our lives and circumstances are orchestrated in such a way that we "would seek him [God] and perhaps reach out for him and find him, though he is not far from any one of us."[4] I once overheard someone in our church foyer say: "I wish God would speak to me the way he speaks to you." I quickly responded: "That desire you have to hear from God is God speaking to you." It is here that we need to help people grow: in hearing God through both those first inclinations for hope and then through the trusted words of the Bible. The convergence of these kinds of moments stirs hope that healthy relationships are possible with God's help. When this does not happen, many in our secular age are drawn to strange, esoteric signs, alternative worldviews, and even conspiracies to quench the pain of relational fragmentation.

BROKEN RELATIONSHIPS IN A SELF-HELP WORLD

Recently, the Grammy Award-winning song "Flowers"[5] put its finger on the relational advice many in a secular culture are getting. If you have heard the song, you know it's not only musically catchy, but it talks plainly about a broken relationship. Consider the rawness of these words: "We were right 'til we weren't, built a home and watched it burn. Mm, I didn't wanna leave you." Songs like this point to the zeitgeist of our age and our loss of hope that healthy relationships are even possible. However, the paradox is that though we long for healthy and authentic relationships, we are unsure on

---

4. Acts 17:27.

5. "Flowers," by Miley Cyrus, released as a single by Columbia on January 12, 2023.

The Bible as Guide for Restored Relationships

how to cultivate, grow, and mature into people who can give shape to this kind of wholeness.

Shockingly, the song's solution to this broken relationship is even more isolating, mixed with endless self-help options. The chorus states: "I can buy myself flowers ... write my name in the sand ... talk to myself for hours ... I can hold my own hand ... I can love me better ... " This could not be further from the truth, and we know and feel it in our daily interactions. No one holds their own hand and feels a deep sense of intimacy and belonging. No one writes their name in the sand as a statement of conquering sadness. At its core, songs like this point to an internal conflict that misses out on the vision of healthy relationships while longing for them. Further, it blinds us to the restorative way the Bible offers us hope to go on even when everything around us suggests giving up.[6]

When addressing a church community in the Roman Empire, Paul writes: "Everything that was written in the past was written to teach us, so that through the endurance taught in the Scriptures and the encouragement they provide we might have hope."[7] Rules do not promote hope for our present relationship crisis, period. Conversely, the Bible, when heard properly, is a gift that is meant to stir hope. Those formed by the complexities of a secular age are longing for this as they ask the question, "What is hope?"

In the face of family conflicts, betrayal, or painful abandonment, the answers we long for are rooted in our God-given need for hope. It is here that we learn that there is one who meets us in our pain. Jesus and his ways address both our pain and our longing for hope. It is only he who knows how to make all things new. This truth provides a hope that reminds us that even our most difficult experiences are no match for the inner strength and healing God has in store for us. Embracing this has ramifications for our families, who need hope that things will work out even when our next steps are not clear. I have walked with people who needed hope to know that their worst mistakes were not the final word about who they could become. We all want hope to keep believing that our most difficult relationships can be restored. All of this as a secular age continues to reveal new levels of anxiety, loneliness, and worry that move us into a cycle of isolation and hopelessness. This growing sense of hopelessness may be linked to other

---

6. In no way do I intend to minimize the serious and abusive nature of some relationships that require extended periods of separation.

7. Rom 15:4.

challenges that psychologist Jonathan Haidt explores in his assessment of an increasingly anxious generation. Imagine the life-giving hope when people find out that there is a truth about who we are and what really leads to joy that is so much better than just buying yourself flowers.

FORGETTING WHO WE ARE

In *The Lord of the Rings*, there is a powerful scene that captures how hopelessness thrives in isolation and how heathy relationships matter for our identity and sense of worth. The setting involves Sméagol, who later becomes Gollum, undergoing a destructive life-change emphasized by his name change. This shift in identity is due to a newfound lust for the evil ring to rule all others. This distorted desire to possess the ring which he would soon start to call "precious" is so powerful that he murders his friend for fear that he might take the ring. Gollum then shifts into a slow deformation from reality as he speaks to himself, in a type of bipolar anger. He says, "They cursed us and drove us away. And we wept, precious. We wept to be so alone. And we forgot the taste of bread, the sound of trees, the softness of the wind. We even forgot our own name."[8] A distortion into forgetfulness is linked to the lust for power and a loss of identity.

In the Bible, Jesus' first act of hopeful restoration following the pain of his crucifixion is documented in one of the resurrection stories. It involves Jesus calling one of the women at the tomb by her name. I think there is a rich truth in how the Bible links hope with the fact that we are truly known by God. When I was young, I once got lost in a shopping center. I tried to hide as I cried, hoping that my mom would find me. I can't explain that feeling of hearing her call my name as she got closer to where I was. Similarly, Jesus came near and remains near, making us ever aware of God's love that can counter our culture's forgetfulness and lostness. Many in a secular age have forgotten that their names, their voices, and their unique perspectives all point to our need for relational belonging, a mysterious sense that God knows us in an intimate way. See if you notice the way sadness, hope, and hearing one's name converge in this passage:

> She turned around and saw Jesus standing there, but she did not realize that it was Jesus. He asked her, "Woman, why are you crying? Who is it you are looking for?" Thinking he was the gardener, she said, "Sir, if you have carried him away, tell me where you have

---

8. Jackson, dir., *Return of the King*.

put him, and I will get him." Jesus said to her, "Mary." She turned toward him and cried out in Aramaic, 'Rabboni!' (which means "Teacher").[9]

Believing that God still calls us by name is one of the ways the Bible substitutes a rule-based approach for a relationally driven model. Our names are about our roots and our desires to be known in authentic relationships. This human longing helps us recall our place, our earliest memories of family, our need for community, and a universal human yearning to be interconnected with others.

Helen Li, a graduate student from the University of Toronto, has researched relational fragmentation in emerging secular spaces. The research shows how we now live in a "companionship economy" that demonstrates how relational disconnection has made us more desperate for true companionship. In response to these issues Li has "created a job for herself: She rents out her time, offering companionship for those in need, whether it's joining them for meals, exercising, shopping, travelling or attending medical appointments."[10] I suggest that when we take the Bible seriously, we will sense God's empowerment to act in similar ways as Li. In so doing, may we find new ways to link our deepest longing for relations to God's hope and presence.

It has never been clearer that our secular age will need new approaches to rediscover ways to address our shared human longing for relational connection. I want to suggest that the lasting nature of relational connection must be linked to seeing the Bible as a unique gift for cultivating flourishing relationships. When a rule-based approach remains a default, God's living words of truth are misunderstood and often ignored as rules that shame us for not doing better.

As I meet with people I am noticing how many are showing a surprising desire to be rooted and committed to a longer, bigger story. The promises of a hyper-transient and freewheeling way of life are not all they were cracked up to be. Instead, we have a generation raised on ancestry apps with a new awareness about finding authentic connection to who we are, why we are here, and where we came from. While suspicions about who we can trust remain high, we observe a growing sense and need for a deeper-rooted approach to relationships. Cole Arthur Riley's work points to this awareness. Her writing is masterful as she describes the relationship-deteriorating

---

9. John 20:14–16 (NIV).
10. Xu, "A U of T Grad is Renting Out Her Time," lines 3–5.

ways related to secular struggles and the importance of a rooted spirituality and our human connection. Exploring the enigmas of human flourishing related to race, culture, and faith, she writes, "We need other people to see our own faces—to bear witness to their beauty and truth. God has made it so that I can never truly know myself apart from another person."[11] Her writing was recommended to me by a young adult in our church working out deep and important questions about the church in a secular age. I am convinced the Bible still has something important to say to a new generation and it begins by moving beyond the Bible as a rule book.

GNOSTICS: THE DANGERS OF A DISEMBODIED STORY

Healthy human relationships involve our bodies. It might sound silly to mention something so obvious, but we are living in a time where we will have to make a renewed effort to reaffirm our fleshly bodies as a gift for understanding healthy relationships. Skin and bones, blood and water, bowel moments, and runny noses are part of you and me. The Bible presents our enfleshment as a gift from God. With this, the biblical story assumes we understand and embrace the gift of our bodies because they root us in a unique kind of spirituality of place and presence. We are created to flourish best as rooted enfleshed beings.

This is a crucial issue for dealing with a secular age shaped by digital tools that make it difficult to understand the role of our bodies and their link to healthy relationships. Firstly, we need to acknowledge the extremes where some worship the body while others just hate how they feel in their bodies. One health magazine claimed to be the "Body Bible," highlighting our cultural addiction to the perfect body.[12] Secondly, we are wise to consider the new questions about our bodies and the emerging digital revolution, which continues to push toward disembodied ways to live. In addition to our healthy online social connection there are issues related to transhumanism and algorithmic morality, and advancements in robotics that will need our attention and the Bible's wise counsel.

As we learn to embrace the Bible as God's living words for rooted relationships, we will have to consider new ways to reinforce a particular truth: that our bodies are a gift rooted in God's sacred design that is essential for our relational wholeness. Our God-given responsibility to be co-creators

---

11. Riley, *This Here Flesh*, 81.
12. Samuel, "Body Bible."

The Bible as Guide for Restored Relationships

must also be reclaimed as a sacred call. This involves our need for family, friends, and the faithful ways that God continues his restoring work in and through future generations. We must find creative ways to do this while also acknowledging the special place of singleness or the calling to be celibate.

Whenever we get serious about the Bible and its wisdom for both our relationships and our bodies, we soon find ourselves having to become more familiar with a group of thinkers referred to as gnostics. Gnosticism remain one of the most difficult schools of thought in the early church due to its conflicted views about our human bodies and its unbalanced uses of the Bible.

Without getting too complex, I want to highlight a few issues about gnostics and how their ideas are making a comeback in shaping our shifting secular age. While scholars have noted that there were many diverse groups of gnostics, they all seemed to be in agreement that salvation and freedom involved denying the sacredness of our bodies. This disembodied vision of the human person was also linked to their view of salvation, which involved being freed from one's body. This belief birthed a hyper-spirituality that devalued the role of the body and the story of a God who took on flesh for our salvation.

To be clear, gnostic ideas existed before Christianity started. Nevertheless, early Christians writers noticed that many gnostic thinkers approached spirituality in a way that devalued the rooted nature of humanity. They did this by disconnecting our relational ties from the story of God's goodness as revealed in the earliest stories of the Bible. For gnostics the God of the Old Testament was both bad and complicit in creating the problems in the world, because he was the one who created humans with bodies. This is often considered a dualistic view of life that believes that bodies/our flesh are bad and spirit is good. This is not a biblical idea.[13] Appropriately, Christians rejected such a simplistic view of creation that minimized the special connection to our relationships and our human bodies. This is paramount for experiencing flourishing relationships.

The Greek term *gnosis* means knowledge. It is important to note that this word is used over twenty-five times in the New Testament and can be interpreted as good or bad. Some gnostic teachers used the Bible to push for an approach to knowledge that led to a dangerous distortion. Instead of seeing knowledge as an aspect of being fully human, loved by the God who

---

13. When the Bible uses flesh in a negative way it is referring to the *ways* of the flesh, not our human bodies.

created us, and created us to know and be known by him, they despised the role of the body and claimed it was a hindrance to true spiritual knowledge. The solution they proposed was an interpretation of biblical passages that overemphasized spirit and proposed a *secretive* inner knowledge that led to salvation only for a select few.

In 1931, Carl Jung published a work entitled *Modern Man in Search of Soul*. He hinted at the breakdown of relational rootedness and the gnostic issues still at play today. Addressing the inner complexity of the human person and psychoanalytic theories, he noticed that our quest for the inner self had taken a circuitous path. He observed:

> Not . . . merely of the interest taken in psychology . . . but of the widespread interest in all sorts of psychic phenomenon as manifested in the growth of spiritualism, astrology, theosophy, and so forth . . . We can compare it only to the flowering of Gnostic thought in the first and second centuries of Christ.[14]

This disembodied view of a human was enforced by selecting key passages from the Bible. Gnostics did not entirely ignore or reject the Bible, instead they used it and interpreted it in ways that overemphasized solely spiritual themes, concluding that "true" salvation was related to being set free from one's body. Imagine reading Paul, who writes, "I discipline my body and keep it under control, lest after preaching to others I myself should be disqualified" as a gnostic.[15] Their misuse of the Bible devalue the special role for relationships that require us to be embodied. Think of simple things like intimacy, a hug, a kiss, holding hands. All those things were seen as a weakness of creation. Soon even more problematic issues emerged.

THE BIBLE OF THE JEWS NOT JUST FOR JEWS

The earliest concern of this book was to demonstrate that the Bible is God's living words given to us by a long and rich history that points all the way back to his goodness. God reveals this by calling people, with bodies, to himself. The gnostic approach was more selective about which biblical books they would read because of their hyper-spiritual salvation mindset. Almost all gnostic teachers felt that the Hebrew Bible was bad

---

14. Jung, *Modern Man in Search of a Soul*, 238.
15. 1 Cor 9:27.

The Bible as Guide for Restored Relationships

and problematic. The Jews and their belief in a creator God, who made humans with bodies, was to be rejected. It might surprise you, but a simple search on Amazon will show something called *The Very First Bible*. This is a version of books brought together by Marcion, an early figure influenced by Gnosticism. From what we know he was a shipbuilder, son of a bishop, and gnostic leader, who selected key texts to make up his *own* version of an early Bible. It in fact was one of the earliest attempts to compile key books which might gain traction in the early church. If you take a minute to look at this Bible, you'll notice that he left out the Old Testament and New Testament texts that celebrated the Jewish story of a creator God who is revealed as good. For Marcion, and others like him, creation, which includes our bodies, did not fit into the vision of salvation.

Today, we will have to return to the work of guiding those in a secular age to understand the rich legacy of *both* the Hebrew Old Testament and the New Testament. This will require reclaiming the gift of relational hope that connects the people of God in the Old Testament with those in the New. For many who are not Christians yet, and who do not understand the authority of the Bible, it will be easy to bypass this robust and rooted understanding of relational trust informed by a particularly Christian view of history. To ignore this special relational link between the Jews, their Scriptures, and their connection to Jesus is to inch closer to a gnostic approach to the Bible. We must regularly return to the fact that the Old Testament is the Bible that Jesus read, so how could we not have it as our authority to know him and understand his role in fulfilling what it says? This, at its core, is a framework for reading the Bible in light of the hope-filled ways that God was at work through the Hebrew story, making it possible, one day, for people from all nations to also become a part of the family of God.

The gnostic approach to the Bible was dangerous because it made it easy to forget that "The New Testament writers were Old Testament people."[16] This simple phrase captures a vital truth that goes further than a personal view of relationships. In fact, it is a way to draw those in our secular age out of a myopic, me-only view of life. We are created to belong to a larger family that existed long before we were here. Accordingly, this long-relational essence of the Bible is lost when we think of the Bible as old rules we can take or leave as we please. Consequently, a common confusion sets in, informed by hyper-spiritualized interpretations detached from the larger place in God's story. Inadvertently, a tidal wave of private

---

16. Le Peau, *Mark Through Old Testament Eyes*, 9.

spiritualities, using a gnostic interpretive lens, soon leaves those in a secular age open to numerous misunderstandings.

If we hope to reacquaint people with the Bible in a way that includes hopeful insights for flourishing relationships, we must return to this special connection related to the Hebrew Bible, the Jewish people, and the early church's insights related to gnostics. The Bible is not a rule book of laws that fall from the sky, secretively put together by a group of power-hungry leaders. Nor is it secret rules for a select few that get what true spirituality is about. It is the result of humble and patient discernment with a constant reminder of God's desire to have a relationship with his creation. For God's human creation, with bodies as well as souls, this means we are not alone, and that God knows what is needed to restore our sinful and broken world.

As early Christians pushed back against a gnostic reading, they found new ways to reiterate that the spiritual life always includes a valuable appreciation of our bodies. We hug, we cry, we hold hands, we need sleep, and one day Jesus will say "eat and drink, this is my body and blood broken for you." In the context of worship, the Bible speaks of the special, intimate connection of human touch in greeting others with a kiss. Five times in the New Testament this practice is encouraged.[17] It is an act of intimate relational love meant to recall that Judas's kiss does not get the final say about what kissing and human friendship and relational wholeness can mean for us.

The gnostic readings and interpretations were deemed unacceptable because they devalued the truth about who we are as it squeezed the hope of restored relationship out of the Bible. Similarly today, we must address this blind spot that needs correction if we hope to understand the gift of whole and healthy human relationships. While old secular narratives assumed the world was edging toward atheism, something much more complex awaits. We are wise to prepare for a new kind of Gnosticism that will only be countered with sustained imagination of the Bible and relentless attention to God's gift of hope, pointing to our deep longing for restored relationships.

---

17. Rom 16:16; 1 Cor 16:20; 2 Cor 13:12; 1 Thess 5:26; 1 Pet 5:14.

The Bible as Guide for Restored Relationships

YOUR "TRUE SELF": AUTHENTICITY AND ACCOUNTABILITY

On the heels of the gnostic challenges, the shift of this secular culture will accelerate the turn inward that is often captured by phrases like "be your true self." This is a painful cycle of relational roulette that makes it impossible to both define "the self" and to not feel unsettled around the messy realities of relational existence. In a world aggressively against being told what to do, the inner self-assessing voice of private spirituality promises to give us the truth. However, some are starting to learn it never delivers. Considering this, we must create new ways to present biblical promises about our need for rooted relationships that provide a robust understanding of the self. This must include a gentle but firm warning that our feelings *alone* are not always reliable in assessing what is wrong, what we must do, and what is most important for experiencing relational wholeness.

The Bible speaks about the idea of "the self" in a way that is difficult for modern thinkers to understand. In fact, it does so by holding together a vision of our true self that may involve suffering. For those in a secular age, the self is ideally the place where no anxious or painful realities are present. It will come as a surprise to learn what we are actually most ourselves when we learn to embrace and even carry burdens that extend beyond us. Here, the words of Jesus are essential. As he told his earliest followers, "If anyone would come after me, let him deny himself and take up his cross and follow me."[18] While no one saw this coming, it remains living truth that cuts through the self-serving ways of every age. To deny ourselves is not to reject our bodies but to remember they have limits. Hence, the Jesus-shaped version of "the self" involves bearing a cross and embracing the strength to follow him into the life we are meant to live. Put another way, no one finds their true self by just focusing on themselves.

Although Jesus came to bear *the* cross, his obedience makes it possible for us to bear *a* cross. I have always been tempted to look for the shortcut that involves an easy way out. At their worst, today's offers of true spirituality often promise no suffering and endless success. Again, reading the Bible properly can set us free if we slow down to see the relational connectivity that involves those around us. Here we are developing a strength to listen to those who hurt, sit with those who suffer, and acknowledge our relational

---

18. Matt 16:24.

need for friendship and compassion. Even Jesus longed for this, although he didn't need it the way we do.

As we creatively reintroduce the Bible to those formed in this secular age, we must help them see how those in the Bible assumed a completely different understanding of "the self." It is one of the biggest challenges of our time. A first step is to remember that one's true self is only revealed to us to with others in relationships we trust. This involves celebration when others discover new purposes, dreams, hopes, and so on. No one in biblical times would have imagined doing that without the close-knit relationships of family and friends, which included the extended family and their new church family.

Imagine that everyone in the Bible heard about the hope of their true selves alongside others. Subsequently, they would learn that even their success was linked to blessings of others. A stark biblical warning states: "Teach those who are rich in this world not to be proud and not to trust in their money, which is so unreliable. Their trust should be in God."[19] Trust in God pointed to a new awareness of those who God loves, especially the poor. While even those in our secular age are open to generosity and care for the poor, the fabric of relationships offered in the Bible goes further than a handout to help. It involves seeing those around us as brothers and sisters who can build their lives on the truth of Jesus their older brother, the only begotten Son. It involves a whole new understanding of relationship restoration.

This vision of flourishing relationships provides a vision of accountability to God for how one loves others. Imagine hearing "Teach those who are rich . . ." read aloud where both rich and poor are seated side by side as family, in the same church. There might have been some snickers and a few "I told you so" comments around the room. Again, no one in Bible times just opened their Bible or turned to a book to hear things only for themselves. They discovered the life they were meant to live with and among others who were seeking with them God and his hope-filled ways. We need this vision of the Bible linked to relational wholeness to protect us for the onslaught of a consumeristic lens: a distortion that presents spiritual tips to grow one's business, improve one's marriage, or find one's destiny detached from deeply rooted relationships that reveal God's restoring ways for all.

This distorted use of the Bible requires correction if we hope to see our wounded world and reimagine the trusted relationships the Bible promises.

---

19. 1 Tim 6:17 (NLT).

The Bible as Guide for Restored Relationships

The living truth we hear from the Scripture is meant to guide our relationships by telling us the truth about the things that will disorder our interactions with each other. This brings us face to face with a true and trustworthy view of our authentic self and our need for accountability to others as well.

Why did the early Christians trust these writings? One reason is that the documents in our Bible were recognized and affirmed due to their rooted fabric in relational trust. The writers, the carriers, and the communities that gathered to hear them read sensed God's power and presence as they embodied the biblical truth in proximity to each other. This evidential power made visible in community was a sign of rooted trust and sacrificial living that was seen as essential to passing on the faith to others. As the Bible was heard it created new paths for restored trust that others found attractive, realizing they could never achieve it in an isolated search for self-authenticity. Imagine that in just a few years, Pharisees who were part of a group who distrusted Jesus, found themselves now present at the Council of Jerusalem in Acts 15. This is a picture of relational healing and renewed unity for the sake of Jesus and his emerging kingdom.[20]

I am convinced that the gospel of Jesus is able to preserve while it creates. This seems like a paradox in our culture that, again, sees things through a binary lens. Defend or die, win or lose. The good news is that Jesus reveals something altogether different. His living truth was that we discover the life we were meant to live when we die to ourselves and self-centered desires. Surprisingly, this is also the way to strengthen our relationships. I have seen in my own marriage how when I think less of myself something special happens, which encourages my wife and kids in deeper ways. I am learning that the kind of reliable and restoring relationships the Bible offers must be modeled for those in our secular age. In so doing, we help others hear how the trustworthy words of the Bible are so much more than rules. Further, people start to see that our secular age is no match for a church committed to cultivating relational trust, a restoring trust meant to help us love one another, to watch out for disunity, and even to love and pray for those who persecute us.

---

20. In Acts 15:5, the fact that the Pharisees are present at this council and embracing the truth of Jesus cannot be missed.

THE BIBLE FOR A *SHIFTING* SECULAR AGE

HOW JESUS DECONSTRUCTS A RULES APPROACH

Remember the gnostic dislike for fleshly bodies, and imagine how they felt about the idea that Jesus, the divine eternal Word of God, puts on flesh. Yes, they again reverted to their own interpretation, which argued that Jesus was not really God in the flesh. The promise of God with us, for gnostics, was a quasi-God almost like us. Further, the God of the Bible who not only formed us for relationship with himself but also for relationship with each other morphed into something else. To correct this would require urgent attention.

For gnostics, Jesus, the incarnate one, only pretended to have a real body. For them, Jesus' "true self" was just a spiritual essence *trapped* in a body, which was bad.[21] The language of emanations was often used to speak of the levels of spiritual realms, recognizing Jesus for being in the highest realm. For gnostics, Jesus in a body made him weak, and linked to the supposedly inferior God of the Old Testament. Remember that when the earliest biographies of Jesus were recognized as authoritative, they were adamant to describe Jesus with a body, who also experiences aspects of human weakness that the devil tries to capitalize on. This pattern has not changed. In moments of weakness, you and I are most prone to wonder about God's loving ways and whether our relationships can hold together.

In Matthew's version of the temptation story, we read that the devil approaches a *hungry* Jesus with diverse tests. At one point the devil quotes from the Bible. Yes, you read that right. The devil quotes Psalm 91. It states: "If you are the Son of God, jump off! For *the Scriptures say*,[22] 'He will order his angels to protect you. And they will hold you up with their hands, so you won't even hurt your foot on a stone.'"[23] If you go back to read Psalm 91:11-12, you'll see that the devil did a good job. He is right about what the psalmist says, however he stops before the next verse that speaks about what God's protection is for and what one's feet are meant to do. Isn't this the problem? Similarly, we tend to quote a part of the Bible and miss its larger message. We develop the habit of using the Bible when it might help us get our way, never getting honest about the inconvenience to address what God wants to teach us.

---

21. The discovery of the Gospel of Judas remains formative for this debate.
22. My emphasis.
23. Matt 4; Ps 91:11-12.

The Bible as Guide for Restored Relationships

The next verse from Psalm 91 states that the feet that God protects will "tread on the lion and the cobra; you will trample the great lion and the serpent."[24] Satan quotes the Bible in hopes of distracting Jesus from his purpose to conquer sin and death in the mystery of the cross and resurrection. Jesus is not just following rules, he is being obedient because of a deep relational trust with his and our Father. While the devil hopes that Jesus submits to his request, he fails to understand that Jesus also knows verses 12 and 13, which provide the proper and full context. Jesus is living in the promise of a larger relationship.

Those in our secular age have a cultural connection to the Bible that is informed by the shifting ideas we discussed in Part 1 of this book. This shapes how they hear and engage with the Bible if left on their own. Thankfully, the Bible, when read well, takes us to a deeper place. To understand this, let us consider one other key aspect of the temptation story addressed above. No one was with Jesus when this episode with the devil happened. In fact, if you looked at the chronology of it, it takes place before Jesus has even picked his first followers. That means that we only know and have this story about Jesus and the devil quoting the Bible because Jesus would have repeated it to his followers at some point. I like to believe it was Jesus' warning about how easily we might be tempted to misuse the Bible ourselves. We have numerous accounts of it from different perspectives as well, which shows that each writer wants us to see in new ways. Jesus would have told them and reminded them that one can easily abuse the Bible and move others who hear it away from the loving, restoring ways of the Father. It has been my experience that we all may be tempted to use the Bible as a book of rules while remaining ignorant of its truer essence as living words that help us embrace God's restoring ways in all our relationships.

A REVEALING JEOPARDY MOMENT

Philip Yancey nailed it when he wrote, "The more I studied Jesus, the more difficult it became to pigeon-hole him."[25] I hope that as we bring this chapter to a close you are seeing how the same can be said of the Bible. Those in a secular age are depending on us to move beyond presenting the Bible as a rule book you can just ignore. This will require a deeper commitment to relational unity and Christ-centered humility as we get honest about

---

24. Ps 91:13.
25. Yancey, *Jesus I Never Knew*, 23.

conflicts that have the potential to destroy our relationships and the good things God wants to do in our homes, our cities, and our churches.

Recently the internet trending meter had a Bible issue front and center when *Jeopardy* contestants were unable to answer: "Our Father Which Art in Heaven 'this' be thy name."[26] All three contestants remained silent until the buzzer went off. No one knew the answer. What may have seemed like common language from the Lord's Prayer is now a foreign phrase that fewer and fewer people will associate with a loving God. Even more, fewer will know the relational hope that is involved when we pray this prayer with consistency, keeping in mind that the God we pray to has a kingdom that is coming and that we can taste aspects of this coming goodness and love in the most intimate part of life: our relationships.

While it may be tough to turn the tide, I want to propose that we reclaim the Bible as living words that were never meant to be heard and received as just rules in isolation. Because of Jesus, this God we seek to honor is to be understood as a loving father whose guidelines are for the sake of restoring even the most broken relationships. The fact that those who lived in that first century read the Hebrew Bible and still struggled to see how Jesus fit into the larger picture reminds us that we are not immune to the same struggles. However, the shifts and struggles around us will require a firm grasp of God's hope that is extended to others who once felt they could never have a relationship with God.

---

26. McEntyre, "Blasted by Fans for Missing Obvious Bible Answer," para. 2.

Epilogue
Equipping People for the Future: The Church and Our Leadership Crisis

"The greatest problem for the church today is our inability to connect with nonbelievers in a way that they understand... If the church does not identify with the marginalized, it will itself be marginalized. This is God's poetic justice."[1] –Tim Keller

FOR SEVENTEEN YEARS, a local man from Quebec worked on a translation of the Bible into the Mohawk language. I have wondered, what leads people to commit, with such dedication, to certain things that others would consider a waste of time? Gabriel was so moved by hearing the Bible as a youngster that he thought it unthinkable that others should not get a chance to hear the living words of the Bible in a language they understood. When asked about this seventeen-year commitment of translation, he stated: "I kept going because when you start something for the Creator, you can't stop it's so interesting. Every verse is different. I was wondering what the next verse says."[2] I am thankful for servants who, like Gabriel, are ready to keep going in the face of challenges, discouragement, and sheer hard work.

In this last chapter, I want to address a deep shift related to the Bible and leadership. While many of the themes in the previous chapters assume the importance of leading well, we find ourselves in the midst of a leadership crisis that I believe is linked to our shallow engagement with the Bible. It has been my experience and conviction that we must return to the Bible

1. Keller, *Center Church*, 224.
2. Lowrie, "Mohawk-Language Bible Published After Decades-Long Effort," para. 9.

if we hope to lead our way out of the present church crisis. A secular culture has shone a light on the fact that we have not allowed the Bible and the serious work of spiritual leadership to fully penetrate our hearts and renew our minds. Moreover, we now know that a new generation has no vision for what Godly leadership might imply.

At the outset of this book, I proposed that some of cultural shifts in our emerging secular age require a new vision of the Bible and its importance. The world we anticipated did not materialize as we thought. Instead, the secular landscape ahead will be both more challenging and more open to new possibilities for engaging others about faith in Jesus and the Bible. This will inevitably include a major paradigm adjustment concerning spiritual leadership. One of the tasks of a spiritual leader is to be prayerful as they assess present realities without becoming alarmists. As I consider my present context a little "into the future," I have thought of this book as a time machine made of paper. The shifts we are facing are palpable and I am convinced that the Bible remains both sacred and authoritative for forming leaders for the shifts of an emerging secular age. Nevertheless, there is a growing tension that some will miss the good things God may have in store because they have not linked the Bible and what it says about the importance of leadership.

Consider the wisdom the prophet Isaiah wrote about at a time when dire hopelessness led people to fear the burden of leadership.

> People will oppress each other—man against man, neighbor against neighbor . . . A man will seize one of his brothers . . . and say, "You have a cloak, you be our leader; take charge of this heap of ruins!" But in that day he will cry out, "I have no remedy . . . *do not make me the leader of the people.*"[3]

Isaiah puts his finger on something we are sensing in our own time. This is to hear the Bible as living words. More and more people are unsure about leadership and overwhelmed with the challenges ahead. I think this is one of the reasons we are quick to embrace conspiracy beliefs that move us further and further from trusting God and the Bible. While these theories may promise a clear understanding of what is "really" going on, they only reinforce our need for control. To counter such things, we will need a new vision of leadership rooted in the Bible so that we can see through this present storm. While some remain skeptical, I believe that a consistent engagement with the Bible reminds us that we can lead in a way that will

---

3. Isa 3:5–7, emphasis mine.

get us out of the mess we find ourselves in. Just as in other areas, the field of leadership modeled by top-down approaches are fading right before our eyes. Further, a secular age has exposed that talking about leadership is not the same as developing a new kind of leader who will know how to rethink old assumptions about our culture, the church, and the Bible. This, I suggest, is our most urgent task, and I am convinced the Bible has what we need to lead, not just to comment on and bemoan all the challenges ahead.

The Scriptures provide numerous examples of how God raised up leaders for new seasons of change. Reading the Bible with a fresh perspective, as I have suggested, is not the only answer, but my hope is that it can help us shine new light on what is at stake if we miss this opportunity. Moreover, the kind of leaders we will need will have to demonstrate a particular maturity for how to think about the complex realities of the church and the future. In previous chapters, I hinted at the unique communal space of the local church for hearing the Bible read with others, which will remain essential and unmatched as the place of authentic encounters linked to accountability. In a similar fashion, leadership detached from consistent accountability and awareness can create a culture that spirals out of control, leaving a trail of pain.

In this last chapter, I want to focus on the sacred work of leadership within the life of the church that, in many ways, should preoccupy us more than what happens in our world. I often suggest that even a glancing look at church history that reveals that the issues and challenges *in* the church have done more damage to the witness of Jesus than the complex issues *outside* the church. By now you know that I do not like the language of *inside* and *outside*, since a secular age has blurred the lines and impacted all of us no matter where we stand. Nevertheless, I believe our gathered places of worship must be reclaimed as unique spaces to model and grow leaders formed by a faithful engagement with the Bible, as we listen and learn how the church has navigated change in the past.

THE INTERGENERATIONAL FABRIC THAT FORMS LEADERS WHO GET IT

Numerous letters we have in our Bible were written to address the special ways that worship and leadership converged. To our surprise, we do not get simplistic answers but guidelines for seeking holiness, celebrating leadership, and developing a culture of spiritual maturity. The churches we meet through the pages of the Bible were not perfect, but they do reflect that leadership is essential, especially in disruptive times of change. As we read the Bible we are invited to embrace the power of the Holy Spirit to do in us now what he has always done for those who have taken his inspired words seriously. In Acts 2 we see a move of God we might consider the first revival of the church. While many celebrate the power of Pentecost, few notice that this unmatched blessing of God would require a totally different kind of leader. All that is to say that we should never forget that if we pray for revival, we better also pray for leaders who can navigate a church council meeting such as we find in Acts 15.

I recently spoke to a young guest who had never been to a church before. A friend had invited her, and she happily agreed to see what church was all about. As we spoke, I could tell she felt awkward and nervous, yet God had drawn her to visit us on this particular morning. I remember she asked, "Why do people raise their hands when they sing?" Assuring her that it was a great question, I explained that the nature of Christian worship is a *whole body* experience. This intrigued her. Moreover, she was shocked to see both young and old learning together and caring for each other. We may have taken it for granted but it may shock some to see the intergenerational space within church that provides a unique context where biblical wisdom can inform how we develop future leaders.

Leadership sage Warren Bennis once remarked, "Effective leaders put words to the formless longings and deeply felt needs of others. They create communities out of words."[4] The Bible gives us the words we need to create communities that will grow leaders that the world so desperately needs. It also warns us of what is at stake if we miss such a sacred calling. Even though leaders are formed in diverse spaces in society, it has been my experience that a local church is the most mysterious and meaningful context for addressing our growing leadership crisis—let alone the fact that Jesus told us that he would continue to build his church. Future leaders formed within the mystery of this community Jesus is building model being centered on words of the Bible as we listen to the concerns of a hurting world. As one author rightly remarked, "Mystery is not the absence of meaning, but the presence of more meaning than we can comprehend."[5]

As we have seen, the language of mystery suits those in a secular age exploring diverse spiritual issues. Moreover, mystery and leadership

---

4. Bennis, *Managing the Dream*, 282.
5. Covington, *Salvation on Sand Mountain*, 203–4.

Epilogue

converge to remind us that we must think about preparing spiritual leaders for a world that does not yet exist. This should include the wisdom of older and more experienced leaders who know how to make room for new and younger ones. Mutual loving and mutual learning is at the core of the church models provided for us in the Bible. I would add that we can celebrate the joy of faithful *hand-offs*. While the Bible does not give us an exact science for handing over leadership to the next generation, it is an assumption for those who know that the kingdom of Jesus will have no end.

In his letter to the church in Philippi, Paul provides wisdom for leadership linked to future possibilities, all along reminding us that Jesus has more to teach us. Having committed to have the mind of Christ, he writes:

> Therefore, my dear friends, as you have always obeyed—not only in my presence, but now much more in my absence—continue to work out your salvation with fear and trembling, for it is God who works in you to will and to act in order to fulfill his good purpose.[6]

I return often to this passage as I reflect on my leadership calling. I find that it holds together a call to the church, the unique nature of work, and the mysterious fabric of worshipping a holy God, as well as the increasing benefits of our salvation in an attitude of mysterious reverence.

It seems clearer than ever that those in a secular age are drawn to visit, explore, and even attend our gatherings if mystery, spirituality, and leadership are modeled in a way that is authentic and explained. This can and should be a space to explore new opportunities to reimagine a healthy balance for working out (not to be confused with working for) our salvation as part of a worshipping community of faith. Paul is hopeful that the church in Philippi will prioritize this work of spiritual maturity even if he is not with them, watching over their every move. In so doing, Paul remarks that our worship should improve our ability to recognize God's work in and through us.

May we never forget that God's purposes are linked to working *out* our salvation for the sake of the world. Leaders who get this are the ones who are best positioned to engage in a secular age as they look for examples of working, walking, and wrestling through life while attentive to a God who is ever present, revealing his good and perfect will to us. John Wooden, the legendary leader and famous basketball coach, allegedly remarked, "It is what you learn after you know it all that counts." I cannot help but imagine that "working out our salvation" is an overflow of what we already know,

6. Phil 2:12–13.

shining a light on things we didn't see before. In a secular age, spiritual leadership will include the joy and conviction that God has more light to shine on our present quandaries if we would just recenter around the Bible.

WORK AND WORSHIP: FOUR PRACTICES TO INCREASE BIBLICAL LITERACY

For years, I have tried to teach from the Bible with an awareness that I had a responsibility to develop leaders who would grow a deeper hunger to read the Bible more consistently. Leading a church plant taught me that at any given point I must remember that I am teaching the Bible to a diverse group of people. Some are unsure, curious, hurting, and seeking—all are listening to what the Bible might say to them. A mentor instilled this value in me when he said, "Dom, at the end of the sermon people should not say: 'oh, that was a good talk' but 'how can I learn more about this Jesus?'" Paul's instruction to a young leader in a worship setting rings even more true to me today: "Do your best to present yourself to God as one approved, a worker . . . who correctly handles the word of truth."[7]

As I have thought about how to keep growing in this important biblical wisdom, I have come around to four key practices. These have been a guide as I hold together our need for the Bible and the importance of leading into new and unknown areas. With a deep conviction that the Bible remains essential in a secular age, I try to think of younger leaders in my context who will need encouragement as they develop their own voices for leading through the shifts ahead.

I think our present crisis of leadership is intricately linked to biblical illiteracy. The Bible has leadership wisdom written all over it, however it is easy to miss if we make the Bible a private devotional guide just for our personal goals and dreams. As we will see below, the sheer gift of having a Bible itself requires a leadership network that many rarely consider. The work of getting parchment, paying for copies, traveling to share the letters, and the numerous translations all depended on leaders. Hence leadership and worship are essential categories for expounding the Bible with a changing culture in mind. The four practices I want to explore in detail are these:

I. Biblical clarity that increases a sense of mystery.

II. Genre, grammar, and gratitude.

[7]. 2 Tim 2:15.

Epilogue

III. Weave in the essential doctrines often.

IV. The difference between interpretation and opinions.

I. Biblical clarity that increases a sense of mystery

Whenever we teach from the Bible, we should remind listeners that we enter a mystery, a dialogue with the living God. No one encounters this living God without a new awareness that he offers transformation and not just information. When we inspire people to engage with the Bible in this way, they realize that the goal is not just what is relevant *for them,* but what is required *of them.* We need people to get comfortable with the fact that clarity, according to the Bible, does not mean comfort as it is often presented in our culture. In fact, leaders know that the most important times of maturation happen when we deal with uncomfortable surprises. This provides an increased attention to the mystery that God's ways are beyond our own and that we depend on his strength to lead well.

The master of this approach to teaching and leading was Jesus himself. Parables, his preferred mode of engaging with his listeners, often left them with more questions than answers. In some ways, leaders of the future will have to return to this method as they revisit the Bible with and for others. We must consider how to invite others into a mystery of following, not just believing. Over the years I have found many in our secular spaces who do not read the Bible and who are just learning to explore the deeper things of faith. Their initial motivation to engage with the Bible is linked to a need for relief or peace. Yet, I also remind them that they are not alone when they feel unsure about the next steps God has. The truth of every biblical encounter involves learning to how to trust this mysterious loving God who is calling us to discover the life we were meant to live.

The writers of the Bible share lessons by providing multilayered stories of people who learned to listen, think, pause, follow, and step into the mysterious new opportunities where God was at work. Why would we expect anything different today? Imagine the mystery we enter into when we hear and respond to this sacred invitation:

> Come, all you who are thirsty, come to the waters; and you who have no money, come, buy and eat! Come, buy wine and milk without money and without cost . . . Listen, listen to me, and eat

what is good, and you will delight in the richest of fare. Give ear and come to me; listen, that you may live.[8]

"Come" remains a true way to think about an experience with God that awakens leadership awareness. It also requires attention to make sure we do not confuse mystery with the strange feelings some equate with mysticism. This will require our attention, yet we cannot silence our need for an encounter with God. When we respond to God's invitation to come, we model for others the unique context of the church as others learn to lead alongside us. There are hardly any example of Jesus just sitting one on one alone with an individual. In fact, the examples we do have are seen as odd.[9]

II. Genre, Grammar, and Gratitude

A pastor invited his church to come ready for next Sunday's teaching. He asked if they'd read Mark 17 as part of the week's preparation. The following week, at the start of the sermon he asked, "Who took the time to read Mark 17?" Many raised their hands. To his surprise he even heard an amen from the back of the room. After a pause he told the church that the Gospel of Mark ends at chapter 16. He then opened his Bible and began a sermon on the theme of lying.

The larger structure, chapter, section, and pericope point to modes of reading and learning that depend on recognizing the genres of writing within the Bible. We can no longer assume people know a parable is "made up," yet a historical narrative in the book of Chronicles is real. Further, we cannot assume people will appreciate the complex structure of the whole Bible. Just making mention that each book has chapters, verses, and key endings that do not match with others in the Bible is an important conversation that, if not addressed, often leads to doubts. In French, the word for *library* contains the word *Bible* in it. You might know it: *bibliothèque*. The Bible is a library of books complied into one canon and that involves patience to embrace different ways of reading and understanding it.

Accordingly, to understand the Bible better, we need to lead people to appreciate each section requires a different interpretive grid. A proverb is not a parable, and a historical narrative is not a lament or a prayer. It may

8. Isa 55:1–3 (NIV).

9. See John 3 and 4—Nicodemus meeting with Jesus secretly at night for fear of what others would say. Or consider the women at the well, which involved a taboo encounter that the disciples make mention of.

Epilogue

seem simple, but it will be essential to reconnect people to diverse genres, grammar structures, and chronological nuances as we share from the Bible. The past few years have demonstrated to me that even those who have read the Bible for years forget that the imagery of prophetic writers does not fit neatly our modern view of symbols and signs. For this reason, people rush to interpret every change in culture as a secret code about the end of time. Not only is this unwise, but leaders with pastoral sensitivity are needed to correct it and encourage a better way.

To genre and grammar issues we add the sheer chronological nuances. It often shocks people to learn that Paul's letters to churches were written before the Gospels. Our modern fascination with chronological perspectives informed by a modern view of time was not that important to those passing on the Bible as we have it today. Most likely, the earliest Gospel was Mark. Yes, it is not in chronological order in the New Testament (it is preceded by Matthew, which was written later than Mark). Leading and interacting with the large questions of the structure of the Bible puts people in our churches and those in a secular age in a posture of learning and relearning for the sake a larger goal: biblical engagement.

The awareness of multiple translations, grammar, syntax, and genres should be noted for people in order to awaken a deeper sense of gratitude. God, from the beginning of time, has always used leaders and their sacrificial *work* that culminated in the Bible we enjoy today. An informed gratitude is key to a growing engagement with a Bible that many may take for granted. Moreover, whenever we re-engage people with this truth, we should also invite them to consider a similar call to sacrificial work for the sake of those who still do not have a Bible or are not sure how to get started as they read it for the very first time.

III. Weave in essential doctrines often

A few months ago, I gave a talk at a leading university in our city. At a student group's invitation, I was asked to address themes related to the Bible. They had questions about who selected the books, the timeline, and translations—all relevant for understanding the Bible better for today. Surprisingly, many students who asked questions were Christians. One student waited until the end and in an embarrassed fashion said, "Why didn't we learn any of this in church?"

I remember her sense of disappointment for not having engaged with questions about the Bible sooner. While I didn't know the answer to that, I had a sense that many leaders do not engage to explore the Bible through a rich historical framework. Put another way, there is no book in the Bible on the importance of the historical guidelines for the gift of the Bible. The early followers of Jesus assumed it was an overflow of Old Testament references to the Law. Consider this Old Testament prayer: "I have hidden your word in my heart that I might not sin against you."[10] Into the New Testament period Paul's own letters were circulating and they too were regarded as containing some difficult ideas. As we read in 2 Peter:

> Just as our beloved brother Paul also wrote to you according to the wisdom given him, as he does in all his letters . . . There are some things in them that are hard to understand, which the ignorant and unstable twist to their own destruction, as they do the other Scriptures.[11]

Christian historian Justo Gonzalez has written an exceptional book on the Bible in the early church. He notes: "Accepting the authority of the sacred books of the people of Israel, they [early Christians] would now read them from a different perspective."[12] This different perspective included revisiting their doctrinal framework related to monotheism, worship, holiness, the temple, and many other beliefs. This required careful attention to other doctrines as their new interpretations attempted to make sense of Jesus as both suffering servant and victorious, risen Lord and Messiah.

When people start re-engaging the Bible, I have noticed that they may twist some of its truths out of ignorance and uncertainty. This will require gentle correction that makes room to reaffirm doctrines alongside a more faithful reading of the Bible. It is in this moment that we turn people's attention to the doctrinal fabric of our earliest creeds as formative boundary markers about who Jesus was as the eternal only begotten and a person of the Trinity. It will be the work of those in leadership to do so without overwhelming people just getting started. An example might help.

We recently saw an influx of people ready to be baptized in our church. As we revisited Jesus' baptism, we spoke about the larger Hebrew story of God's people who stepped out in faith to be baptized by John the Baptist. Although their baptism was an act of repentance, we must not forget that

---

10. Ps 119:10.

11. 2 Pet 3:15–17.

12. Gonzalez, *Bible in the Early Church*, 121.

many of those baptized by John were already part of God's covenant people as Jews. However, when the Bible speaks of Jesus' baptism we must read with an awareness of some new doctrinal markers. In Matthew's Gospel we read:

> As soon as Jesus was baptized, he went up out of the water. At that moment heaven was opened, and he saw the Spirit of God descending like a dove and alighting on him. And a voice from heaven said, "This is my Son, whom I love; with him I am well pleased."[13]

You might have noticed the imagery and language that sheds light on early reference to a Christian understanding of God's nature as a Trinitarian God. Notice here the voice of God the Father, the presence of God the Holy Spirit, and the obedience of God the Son. This narrative oozes with doctrinal points that we need to pause to point out if we hope people will learn to read their Bible in ways that will mature them as spiritual leaders. In doing this, we weave in important Christian doctrines as a lens to understand the Bible as we give people a new awareness of what they should look for when they are reading their Bible alone.

This use of the Bible lets listeners come to appreciate the plain reading of the passage, and the larger doctrinal lens that is also there. When we pause to acknowledge moments like this, those who hear the Bible in a secular age get drawn into the rich and robust theological fabric of the Christian faith that they often assume is shallow and unintelligent. While it will likely lead to more questions, it is still a crucial space for exploring and explaining the faith in new ways.

IV. The Difference Between Interpretations and Opinions

For many in a secular age, diverse interpretations may often be confused with opinions. This is a default posture of most people who assume that every opinion and interpretation is equally valid. Leading well while keeping the Bible in mind requires that we help people develop an awareness that the future of leadership can unintentionally only add to a "that's-my-opinion" approach. In my experience, I have seen leaders ignore this and soon people conclude no one really knows what the Bible means, thus it cannot be trusted as authoritative. This is an important issue that every, and I mean

13. Matt 3:16–17.

every, future leader will have to work through while moving through our present church crisis. At its core we must develop a practice that involves celebrating diverse *reliable* interpretations and not confusing that with an array of *private* opinions.

The Bible states that, in this life, we never get a perfect picture pertaining to all matters of faith. However, this does not mean we don't know any of the picture. The greatest work on biblical interpretation of the early church, if not to the present day, is called *On Christian Doctrine*. In it, St. Augustine writes, "Whoever takes another meaning out of Scripture than the writer intended, goes astray, but not through any falsehood in the Scripture."[14] This doesn't mean that there is only "one" reading of the Bible, Augustine himself offers many. However, of the many there are some that are false. This should keep us mindful that there is a difference between what we fully understand versus an opinion that may move us down a path of falsehoods. It will take leadership to demonstrate that we can celebrate the trustworthiness of the Bible for what is essential for salvation, even as we struggle to understand it more fully.

Throughout this work Augustine addresses the natural and unnatural ways we may stray from the most reliable interpretation of a biblical text. Only when we embrace the Bible as authoritative do we learn to keep returning to it to learn, grow, and even revise our opinions for more trusted interpretations. This requires humility prompted by wisdom as we get honest about the challenges we face as leaders. In a secular age, it is paramount to do so as we admit that we are all prone to preferred interpretations. Some of this is linked to a denominational lens that may be overemphasizing a particular, distinctive historical period. While this is not necessarily wrong, leaders must do better, stating other views of a passage without belittling other reliable interpretations presented by serious and faithful Christians. To fail to do so only confuses those listening, and that models an arrogant attitude rather than a humble one.

In a secular age, this nuanced approach makes room for a crucial dialogue with the global church, correcting years of an imbalanced Western-centered reading of the Bible. A growing church that takes leadership and the future seriously recalls how the church, as it expanded, read and learned that each part of the body brought important perspectives. In some sense, this practice is about how we return to the simple idea that the Bible is the

---

14. Augustine, *On Christian Doctrine*, 533.

Epilogue

infallible and inspired word of God, but our interpretations are not. This will bring to the forefront that the Bible doesn't belong to just one group of people, or one denomination, or even one country. Rather it is God's word for all people, at this time and throughout time, and more than ever in these changing times.

Opinions may not be bad or wrong, but they do not carry the gravitas meant to anchor others who are just learning to read and study the Bible well. In his important book *Whose Bible Is It Anyway?*, the late Jaroslav Pelikan reminds us that while the Bible belongs exclusively to none of us, it addresses all of us. The more I have grown in my understanding of the Bible, the more I have become aware that the Bible can speak to me, and that doesn't mean an issue is always settled for everyone. Now, I am not talking about essential Bible texts, reinforced by creedal authority respected across all Christian denominations from the earliest days of the faith. These are binding for all, but regular readings of the Bible that are being worked out on the front lines of learning and leading require grace, truth, and patience. Anything else only weakens people's trust in the Bible.

Early on in our church plant I kept repeating: "Christianity did not begin when we became Christians." For many this was a helpful shift in their Bible reading. In fact, one person told me this helped him appreciate the rich layers of interpretation he might have missed in his reading. When we read the Bible well, we step into a living stream of living truth, carrying us toward new possibilities so that Jesus and the power of resurrection are made known to the ends of the earth. While numerous opinions may be helpful, they are not equally valid compared to the passed-on teachings that have been tested for centuries, rooted in the Bible and reaffirmed by Christians in different denominations. Such truth-worthy interpretations should steer our opinions and remind us of our responsibility to one body, diverse and dedicated to Jesus.

These four simple teaching habits have been proven to be very helpful, although I am sure we will discover new ones as well. If it helps, consider them as stepping stones for your context as you notice emerging secular realities that require nuance and imagination. They have helped me elevate the authority of Scripture as I remember that God's mysterious ways are far greater than what we, in this life, can fully comprehend. May we never forget:

For what we preach is not ourselves, but Jesus Christ as Lord, and ourselves as your servants for Jesus' sake. For God, who said, "Let light shine out of darkness," made his light shine in our hearts to give us the light of the knowledge of God's glory displayed in the face of Christ. But we have this treasure in jars of clay to show that this all-surpassing power is from God and not from us.[15]

TWO MEANINGS OF "WONDER": A RESURRECTION-CENTERED CHURCH

I want to conclude by drawing our attention to the way our work and God-honoring worship can produce a new sense of wonder in how we lead through crisis moments. In English the word *wonder* can mean "awe," or it can mean "suspicion." Think about it, "I wonder if they are telling me the truth?" is a common refrain for those in a secular age. The media is lying, the politicians are lying, the books we read are maybe not telling us the whole story. *Who* is behind this agenda?

The biblical narratives around the resurrection hold together these two ways of using the word *wonder*. The earliest accounts of Jesus' death and resurrection point to appearances that were beginning to stir a new sense of wonder and hope that Jesus was in fact alive. While some responded in awe, others develop a plan to get people suspicious in their wondering. According to Matthew's account:

> When the chief priests had met with the elders and devised a plan, they gave the soldiers a large sum of money, telling them, "You are to say, 'His disciples came during the night and stole him away while we were asleep.' If this report gets to the governor, we will satisfy him and keep you out of trouble." So the soldiers took the money and did as they were instructed. And this story has been widely circulated among the Jews to this very day.[16]

Here we read of a type of chaos rooted in the love of money that would add suspicion to news about the resurrection of Jesus. The followers of Jesus were often confused but they had never been grave-robbers, or robbers of any kind. In fact, Jesus himself showed them that he would not stand for anyone who would take advantage of others for the sake of money when he flipped tables as a symbol of sacred cleaning of the temple, accusing the

---

15. 2 Cor 4:5–7.
16. Matt 28:12–15.

religious leaders of being thieves. As we consider Matthew's insight about suspicion at the hands of the chief priests, we turn to Luke's perspective for another kind of wonder.

Luke's account reveals a surprising mystery offering us a picture of Jesus that centers our attention on the wonder and mystery of worship. Following the painful fact that Jesus was dead, two of his first followers go back home to the town of Emmaus. Soon, we are told that the resurrected Jesus meets them on the way. As Cleopas and his friend walk home from a stressful few days in Jerusalem, Jesus joins them and listens to their comments as their hopes are shattered. Those in a secular age have their own stories of shattered hope and may in fact be more open than ever to see a different way, if we could learn to listen as Jesus does.

Patiently, Jesus asks Cleopas and his companion a question to help them go deeper and explore their dashed dreams. They say, "We had hoped that he was the one who was going to redeem Israel."[17] This post-resurrection moment reminds us that Cleopas and his friend must learn to see that their previous hopes were just too small for the grandeur bursting forth following the resurrection. Might they be open to see something they had never seen? Might we be ready to return to the Bible and the resurrection hope to wonder, with awe and imagination, that Jesus is meeting us in our doubts to ask us some new questions?

Jesus, consistent with his ways before his death and resurrection, asks questions and at the right time begins to renew the minds of Cleopas and his friend with teaching. As he spoke with them, we are told "and beginning with Moses and all the Prophets, he explained to them what was said in all the Scriptures concerning himself."[18] They, as oral learners, would not have found it difficult to recall by memory key moments from the prophets as part of rethinking the identity of Jesus the Rabbi. Jesus links those pieces for them without telling them who he is just yet.

This is the place where the ancient story of Israel converges with a new chapter flowing out of the cross and resurrection. The pair soon invites this stranger, the resurrected Jesus, to stop and join them for meal. We read, "As they approached the village to which they were going, Jesus continued as if he were going farther. But they urged him strongly, 'Stay with us, for it is nearly evening; the day is almost over.' So, he went in to stay with them."[19]

17. Luke 24:21a (NIV).
18. Luke 24:27.
19. Luke 24:28–29.

Modeling hospitality to a stranger was at the heart of Jesus' message so they acted accordingly. They had listened to Jesus' teaching and now they were ready for more.

Strategically, Jesus "took bread, gave thanks, broke it and began to give it to them. Then their eyes were opened, and they recognized him."[20] There is so much we could pause to say, but I want to suggest that those in a secular age will need consistent moments where we make room for their strange questions and dashed hopes and dreams as we walk them closer and closer to the sacred mystery where Jesus opens their eyes to understand what they could not grasp sooner. It is these lessons of Jesus that will help us lead people back to the sacred Scriptures, as well as our sacred meal that promises his sacred mysterious presence for our ongoing nourishment.

As I have often told our church, Cleopas and his friend immediately do a 180. And 180 is the name of our church for that reason. Jesus is still turning people around as they hear and realize there is something more to his living truth. Later, Cleopas and his friend return to Jerusalem and tell those gathered, "It is true! The Lord has risen . . . Then the two told what had happened on the way, and how Jesus was recognized by them when he broke the bread."[21] Jesus has opened their eyes while also teaching them to return to the Bible. Their despair has turned to wonder and awe as a prerequisite to the kind of leadership Jesus is preparing them for. The Bible, and our engagement with it, is meant to prepare us for the ways God is still meeting us in our doubts and orienting us toward an unknown future. While some are busy conspiring with other plans, Jesus is at work as his people worship him as the living, resurrected Lord.

Might we believe again that a church in crisis will only find its way forward when the Bible, shaped by the resurrection's living words of a living God, becomes our focus again. As this happens, might we believe again that God wants to keep drawing discouraged and disillusioned people into new encounters of worship focused on the resurrected Jesus. Can we lead those who have read the Bible for years to hear it in new ways? In so doing, may those who have not heard of the living ways of Jesus learn that their hopelessness is no match for a Jesus that knows how to revive our need for hope in him. For some it's a path of hope and joy they did not even see was there. This was my story. Maybe it's yours as well.

---

20. Luke 24:30–31.
21. Luke 24:33–35.

Epilogue

An approach to the Bible that can navigate the shifts of a secular age will require that we remain aware of the two types of wonder people carry in their hearts and minds. For those formed by the life-changing words of the Bible, we know that this has always been God's way. For those who remain suspicious and nervous as they wonder if the Bible can truly be trusted, we recall that Jesus has a way. As we remember the tension between the two types of wonder, we must remember that Jesus says to us what he said to his earliest followers navigating unimaginable change: "Peace be with you."[22]

---

22. Luke 24:36.

Bibliography

Augustine. *Confessions.* Translated by Henry Chadwick. Oxford: Oxford University Press, 1991.
———. "On the Catechizing of the Uninstructed." In *The Nicene and Post-Nicene Fathers,* Series 1, Volume 3. Translated by Rev. S. D. F. Salmond. Boston: Hendrickson, 1994.
———. *On Christian Doctrine.* In *Nicene and Post-Nicene Fathers: First Series,* vol. 2, translated by J. F. Shaw, edited by Phillip Schaff, 535–97. N.p.: Christian Literature Publishing Co., 1887.
———. *On Christian Teaching.* Translated by R. P. H. Green. New York: Oxford University Press, 2008.
Aurelius, Marcus. *Meditations.* Translated by Gregory Hays. New York: Modern Library, 2002.
Bantu, Vince. *A Multitude of All Peoples: Engaging Ancient Christianity's Global Identity.* Downers Grove, IL: InterVarsity, 2020.
Barna Group. "The Open Generation: A Global Teens Study." https://www.barna.com/collections/the-open-generation/.
Bauckham, Richard. *Bible and Mission: Christian Witness in a Postmodern World.* Grand Rapids: Baker Academic, 2003.
Bennis, Warren. *Managing the Dream: Reflections on Leadership and Change.* New York: Basic, 2000.
Berger, Peter. "Secularism in Retreat." *The National Interest* 46 (1996/97) 3–12.
Berger, Peter, ed. *The Desecularization of the World: Resurgent Religion and World Politics.* Grand Rapids: Eerdmans, 1999.
Biggar, Nigel. *Colonialism: A Moral Reckoning.* London: William Collins, 2023.
Bird, Natasha. "The Rise Of Modern Stoicism: Is Keeping Calm A Healthy Option?" https://www.elle.com/uk/life-and-culture/culture/a42993347/stoicism-keeping-calm/.
Brague, Rémi. *Curing Mad Truths: Medieval Wisdom for the Modern Age.* Notre Dame: University of Notre Dame Press, 2019.
Bruce, F. F. *Paul: Apostle of the Free Spirit.* Carlisle, UK: Paternoster, 1980.
Brueggemann, Walter. *The Collected Sermons of Walter Brueggemann.* Louisville: Westminster John Knox, 2011.
Bruner, Raisa. "High-Tech Astrology Apps Claim to Be More Personalized Than Ever. Gen Z-ers Are Turning Out to Be Believers." *TIME,* July 23, 2021. https://time.com/6083293/astrology-apps-personalized/.

Bibliography

Callaghan, Shaun, et al. "Feeling Good: The Future of the $1.5 Trillion Wellness Market." McKinsey & Company, April 8, 2021. https://www.mckinsey.com/industries/consumer-packaged-goods/our-insights/feeling-good-the-future-of-the-1-5-trillion-wellness-market.

Calvin, John. *Commentaries, Vol. 6: Psalms 93–150*. Translated by James Anderson. Grand Rapids: Baker, 1989.

Canadian Conference of Catholic Bishops. "Pope Francis' Penitential Pilgrimage." https://www.cccb.ca/indigenous-peoples/pope-francis-penitential-pilgrimage/.

CBC Arts. "Montreal's Historic Reputation as a City of Stained Glass Gets Reworked with a Contemporary Vision." December 29, 2017. https://www.cbc.ca/arts/montreal-s-historic-reputation-as-a-city-of-stained-glass-gets-reworked-with-a-contemporary-vision-1.4463022.

CBC Listen. "How Chess Became the Hottest Game Among Teenagers." *Day 6*, May 5, 2023. https://www.cbc.ca/listen/live-radio/1-14-day-6/clip/15982919-how-chess-became-hottest-game-among-teenagers.

Chadwick, Henry. *The Early Church*. Kindle ed. London: Penguin, 1993.

Clapp, Rodney. *Tortured Wonders: Christian Spirituality for People, Not Angels*. Grand Rapids: Brazos, 2004.

Clarke, Brian, and Stuart Macdonald. *Leaving Christianity: Changing Allegiances in Canada Since 1945*. Montreal: McGill-Queen's University Press, 2017.

Conti, Allie. "Do Yourself a Favor and Go Find a 'Third Place.'" *The Atlantic*, April 4, 2022. https://www.theatlantic.com/family/archive/2022/04/third-places-meet-new-people-pandemic/629468/.

Cosper, Mike. "Bono's Punk-Rock Rebellion Was a Cry of Hopeful Lament." *Christianity Today*, December 2022. https://www.christianitytoday.com/ct/2022/december/bono-book-interview-cover-story-u2-hope-punk.html.

Covington, Denis. *Salvation on Sand Mountain*. New York: Addison-Wesley, 1995.

D'Anastasio, Cecilia. "Chess is Booming Among Teens. Here's Why." Polygon, April 4, 2023. https://www.polygon.com/tabletop-games/23679440/teens-love-chess-memes-boom-2023.

Earls, Aaron. "Most Teenagers Drop Out of Church When They Become Young Adults." Lifeway Research, January 15, 2019. https://research.lifeway.com/2019/01/15/most-teenagers-drop-out-of-church-as-young-adults/.

Fairbairn, Donald. *The Global Church: The First Eight Centuries*. Grand Rapids: Zondervan, 2021.

Fast Company. "Ghosted, Orbited, Breadcrumbed: Digital Dating is Hard. Here's How to Cope." April 29, 2024. https://www.fastcompany.com/91114972/ghosted-orbited-breadcrumbed-digital-dating-how-to-cope.

Ferris, Tim. "How to Apply Stoic Philosophy to Your Life." YouTube, September 12, 2015. https://www.youtube.com/watch?v=AoXxceO4qSo.

Fredricksen, Paula. "Who Was Paul?" In *The New Cambridge Companion to St. Paul*, edited by Bruce Longenecker, 23–47. Cambridge: Cambridge University Press, 2020.

Gerhardt, Megan W., et al. "Harnessing the Power of Age Diversity." *Harvard Business Review*, March 8, 2022. https://hbr.org/2022/03/harnessing-the-power-of-age-diversity.

Gonzalez, Justo L. *The Bible in the Early Church*. Grand Rapids: Eerdmans, 2022.

Bibliography

Greshko, Michael. "Why These Birds Carry Flames in Their Beaks." *National Geographic*, January 8, 2018. https://www.nationalgeographic.com/animals/article/wildfires-birds-animals-australia.

Hagerty, Barbara B. "A Fast Fall For Once Mighty Megachurch." NPR, *All Things Considered*, October 19, 2010. https://www.npr.org/2010/10/19/130679470/a-fast-fall-for-once-mighty-megachurch.

Hanson, Sharon. "The Secularization Thesis: Talking at Cross Purposes." *Journal of Contemporary Religion* 12 (1997) 159–79.

Hauerwas, Stanley. *A Cross-Shattered Church: Reclaiming the Theological Heart of Preaching*. Grand Rapids: Brazos, 2009.

Harari, Yuval Noah, and Pedro Pinto. "Humanity Is Not That Simple." YouTube, June 6, 2023. https://www.youtube.com/watch?v=4hIlDiVDww4&ab_channel=YuvalNoahHarari.

Hart, Kevin. "The Hard Lesson Kevin Hart's Mother Taught Him." YouTube, April 14, 2013. https://www.youtube.com/watch?v=pSN8k8mRJKU.

Hays, Richard B. *Reading with the Grain of Scripture: The Whole Church Reading the Whole Scripture*. Grand Rapids: Eerdmans, 2022.

Hovsepian, Ann-Margret. "Quebec: Canada's Prodigal Province." *Christianity Today*, May 2012, https://www.christianitytoday.com/ct/2012/may/quebec-prodigal-province.html.

Jackson, Peter, dir. *The Lord of the Rings: The Return of the King*. Burbank, CA: New Line Cinema, 2003.

Jeffers, Robinson. "The Treasure." https://poets.org/poem/treasure.

Jung, Carl G. *Modern Man in Search of a Soul*. Translated by W. S. Dell and Cary F. Baynes. Eastford, CT: Martino, 2017.

Keller, Timothy. *Center Church: Doing Balanced, Gospel-Centered Ministry in Your City*. Grand Rapids: Zondervan, 2012.

Koyzis, David T. *Political Visions & Illusions: A Survey & Christian Critique of Contemporary Ideologies*. Downers Grove, IL: IVP Academic, 2019.

Laflamme, Sarah Wilken. "Religion, Non-Belief, Spirituality and Social Behavior among North American Millennials." September 19, 2019. https://uwspace.uwaterloo.ca/handle/10012/15102.

Le Peau, Andrew T. *Mark Through Old Testament Eyes*. Grand Rapids: Kregel, 2017.

Lewis, C. S. *A C. S. Lewis Treasury*. San Diego: Harcourt Brace & Co., 1988.

Louis C. K. *Back to the Garden*. Directed by Louis C. K. Circus King Productions, 2023.

Lowrie, Morgan. "Mohawk-Language Bible Published After Decades-Long Effort by One Quebec Man." CTV News, August 30, 2023. https://montreal.ctvnews.ca/mohawk-language-bible-published-after-decades-long-effort-by-one-quebec-man-1.6540610.

Luhrmann, Tanya. *When God Talks Back: Understanding the American Evangelical Relationship with God*. New York: Vintage, 2012.

Macinnis, Adam. "Report: 26 Million Americans Stopped Reading the Bible Regularly During COVID-19." *Christianity Today*, April 20, 2022. https://www.christianitytoday.com/news/2022/april/state-of-bible-reading-decline-report-26-million.html.

Mansoor, Sanya. "The 'Deplorable' History Behind the Pope's Apology to Canada's Indigenous Communities." *TIME*, July 25, 2022. https://time.com/6200213/pope-apology-canada-history-indigenous-communities/.

Bibliography

Martin, Adam. "Malcolm Browne, 'Burning Monk' Photographer, Dead at 81." *The Atlantic*, August 28, 2012. https://www.theatlantic.com/national/archive/2012/08/malcolm-browne-burning-monk-photographer-dead-81/324221/.

Martinez-Ales, Gonzalo, et al. "Why Are Suicide Rates Increasing in the United States? Towards a Multilevel Reimagination of Suicide Prevention." In *Behavioral Neurobiology of Suicide and Self Harm*, edited by E. Baca-Garcia, 1–23. Current Topics in Behavioral Neurosciences 46. Berlin: Springer, 2020. https://www.ncbi.nlm.nih.gov/pmc/articles/PMC8699163/.

McEntyre, Nicholas. "'Heathen' 'Jeopardy!' Contestants Blasted by Fans for Missing Obvious Bible Answer." *New York Post*, June 15, 2023. https://nypost.com/2023/06/15/jeopardy-contestants-fail-to-answer-bible-clue-about-our-father/.

McGrath, Alister E. *Narrative Apologetics: Sharing the Relevance, Joy, and Wonder of the Christian Faith*. Grand Rapids: Baker Academic, 2019.

———. *What's the Point of Theology?* Grand Rapids: Zondervan, 2022.

McGurk, Stuart. "Making Dreams Come True: Inside the New Age World of Manifesting." *The Guardian*, March 20, 2022. https://www.theguardian.com/lifeandstyle/2022/mar/20/making-dreams-come-true-inside-the-new-age-world-of-manifesting/.

Moati, Raoul. *Derrida/Searle: Deconstruction and Ordinary Language*. New York: Columbia University Press, 2014.

Mosimann, Yasmine. "Reconceptualizing Higher Power(s): Exploring New Religious Movements in Quebec." *The McGill Daily*, March 16, 2015. https://www.mcgilldaily.com/2015/03/reconceptualizing-higher-powers/.

National Geographic. "The Dead Sea Scrolls: 75 Years Since Their Historic Discovery." Special issue, August 2023.

Newbigin, Lesslie. *Foolishness to the Greeks: The Gospel and Western Culture*. Grand Rapids: Eerdmans, 1986.

———. *Is Christ Divided? A Plea for Christian Unity in a Revolutionary Age*. Grand Rapids: Eerdmans, 1961.

Newman, Alex. "Shocking Statistics on Bible Reading." *Faith Today*, May/June 2014, 49–51.

Niebuhr, H. Richard. *Christ and Culture*. New York: Harper & Row, 1951.

Parkin, Hillary G. "The Anxieties and Apps Fuelling the Astrology Boom." BBC, February 8, 2021. https://www.bbc.com/worklife/article/20210205-why-astrology-is-so-popular-now.

Peterson, Eugene. *Eat This Book: A Conversation in the Art of Spiritual Reading*. Grand Rapids: Eerdmans, 2006.

Peterson, Jordan. "Ancient Wisdom at an Ancient Library." YouTube, September 12, 2020. https://www.youtube.com/watch?v=9ByjCwumwBM.

Pew Research Center. "In U.S., Decline of Christianity Continues at Rapid Pace." October 17, 2019. https://www.pewresearch.org/religion/2019/10/17/in-u-s-decline-of-christianity-continues-at-rapid-pace/.

Pieper, Josef. *Abuse of Language, Abuse of Power*. Translated by Lothar Krauth. San Francisco: Ignatius, 1992.

Pigliucci, Massimo. "Stoicism as a Philosophy for an Ordinary Life." TEDxAthens, June 2018. https://www.ted.com/talking/massimo_pigliucci_stoicism_as_a_philosophy_for_an_ordinary_life.

Postman, Neil. *Amusing Ourselves to Death: Public Discourse in the Age of Show Business*. London: Viking, 1986.

Bibliography

Prothero, Stephen. *God Is Not One: The Eight Rival Religions That Run the World*. New York: HarperOne, 2010.

Radosh, Daniel. "The Good Book Business." *The New Yorker*, December 18, 2006. https://www.newyorker.com/magazine/2006/12/18/the-good-book-business.

Rae, Noel. "How Christian Slaveholders Used the Bible." *TIME*, February 23, 2018. https://time.com/5171819/christianity-slavery-book-excerpt/.

Riley, Cole Arthur. *This Here Flesh: Spirituality, Liberation, and the Stories That Make Us*. New York: Convergent, 2023.

Samuel, Ebenezer. "The Body Bible." *Men's Health*, January-February 2024. https://www.magzter.com/stories/health/Mens-Health-US/THE-BODY-BIBLE.

Science Daily. "When Damaged, the Adult Brain Repairs Itself by Going Back to the Beginning." April 15, 2020. https://www.sciencedaily.com/releases/2020/04/200415133654.htm.

Sebek, Petra P. *Spirituality in the Selfie Culture of Instagram*. Eugene, OR: Wipf & Stock, 2019.

Sparrow, Andrew. "Britain Is Now 'Post-Christian', Says Ex-Archbishop Rowan Williams." *The Guardian*, April 27, 2014. https://www.theguardian.com/uk-news/2014/apr/27/britain-post-christian-says-rowan-williams.

Springtide Research Institute. "Gen Z and Religion—What The Statistics Say." https://springtideresearch.org/post/religion-and-spirituality/gen-z-and-religion-what-the-statistics-say.

———. *The State of Religion and Young People 2023: Exploring the Sacred*. https://springtideresearch.org/product/the-state-of-religion-young-people-2023-exploring-the-sacred.

The Straits Times. "Japan Classrooms to Use AI Robots to Help Teach English." August 21, 2018. https://www.straitstimes.com/asia/east-asia/japan-classrooms-to-use-ai-robots-to-help-teach-english.

Swift, Taylor. New York University Commencement Address. May 18, 2022.

Taylor, Charles. *Sources of the Self: The Making of the Modern Identity*. Cambridge: Harvard University Press, 1989.

Thiessen, Joel, and Sarah Wilkins-Laflamme. *None of the Above: Nonreligious Identity in the US and Canada*. New York: New York University Press, 2020.

Thompson, James W. *Christ and Culture in the New Testament*. Eugene, OR: Cascade, 2023.

Venne, Jean-François. "Swearing is a Sacred Affair in Quebec." *University Affairs*, November 7, 2011. https://archives.universityaffairs.ca/news/news-article/swearing-is-a-sacred-affair-in-quebec.

Walls, Andrew F. *Missionary Movements in Christian History*. Maryknoll, NY: Orbis, 1996.

Xu Xiao. "Inspired by the Chinese Trend, a U of T Grad Is Renting Out Her Time to the Socially Anxious and Isolated." *The Globe and Mail*, March 3, 2024. https://www.theglobeandmail.com/canada/article-companionship-service-loneliness/.

Yancey, Philip. *The Jesus I Never Knew*. Grand Rapids: Zondervan, 1995.

Zuckerman, Phil. *Living the Secular Life: New Answers to Old Questions*. New York: Penguin, 2014.

www.ingramcontent.com/pod-product-compliance
Lightning Source LLC
Chambersburg PA
CBHW022119160426
43197CB00009B/1083